A SELF-ACTUALIZA
AND GOALS ACHIEVEMENT PROGRAM

*For Anyone Willing to Be Open to Life's Natural Urge In The Direction of Completion*

# WORKBOOK

# THE POTENTIAL IS WITHIN YOU

ROY EUGENE DAVIS

LAKE RABUN ROAD • P.O. Box 7 • LAKEMONT, GEORGIA • 30552

ISBN 978-0-87707-253-9

 Persons wishing to become involved with this program may contact our office for free informative literature: Center for Spiritual Awareness, P.O. Box 7, Lakemont, Georgia 30552.

If a CD is defective when you receive it, we will replace it without cost to you when you return it. Downloads are available on the CSA website when entire course is purchased.

## Seminar Trainers

It is planned that seminar trainers will share this program in the field. Any person interested in sharing in this capacity should contact Center for Spiritual Awareness directly, giving background information and previous experience.

# CONTENTS

# ORGANIZATION

## The Sections in this Workbook contain:

- Instructional text in outline format
- Self-assessment pages
- Guidelines pages
- Goal Achievement pages
- Commitment or Review pages
- Planning pages

## Correlation:

| Disc Lessons | Workbook | Book |
|---|---|---|
| Without Limits. Self-Realization | Sections 1, 2 | Chapters 1, 2 |
| Creative Use of the Mind. Creative Imagination. | Section 3 | Chapters 3, 4 |
| The Science of Meditation | Section 4 | Chapter 5 |
| Keys to Emotional Wellness. Health & Vitality. | Section 5 | Chapters 6, 7 |
| Relationships. Your Right Place in Life | Section 6 | Chapter 8 |
| Your Right Place in Life. True & Lasting Prosperity | Section 7 | Chapter 9 |
| | Section 8 | Chapter 10 |

# HOW TO USE THIS PROGRAM

*The Potential Is Within You* is one of the most complete spiritual development programs available. To derive benefit, follow the guidelines and suggestions carefully. By doing so, you invite useful change into your life and into your world.

Listen to the Lessons and absorb the messages. Follow the Workbook exercises and fill in the planning forms. Read the text outline between listening sessions to reinforce and to aid learning retention.

At the rate of one session per day, listen to the entire program and attend to the printed forms. This will afford you an overview of the program and give you the opportunity to plan for all areas of your living experience.

Then, at the rate of one theme per week, listen to the Lessons and go over the printed material and forms. Practice the exercises. Listen to *I Accept Fulfillment Now* whenever you like.

After you have gone through the program concentrate on any theme which is needed and proves to be most useful. Or, combine the themes as you go through the "one theme per week" schedule. Cover all of the material but concentrate on areas where work is needed.

The supplemental text can be used whenever you are inclined to reinforce your study and involvement.

# SECTION

## 1.

## Life Without Limitations

# Definitions

**actualize**: to make real or bring into manifestation. Abilities are actualized when they are expressed or demonstrated. Goals are actualized when they are accomplished. Purposes are actualized when they are fulfilled.

- **self-actualization**: removal of mental restrictions for the purpose of experiencing fulfillment of one's potential and talents.
- **dharma:** Sanskrit word meaning to uphold and maintain. Inherent nature and purpose. That which contributes to the evolutionary process. To be in accord with life processes and one's destined path is to fulfill one's dharma.

**enlightenment**: having true knowledge of higher realities.

**God:** a word used to indicate one ultimate Reality or a concept of it.

**God-realization**: direct experience along with knowledge of ultimate Reality and its processes.

**guna**: a quality or attribute of consciousness expressing as a cosmic influence that regulates nature's forces. There are three gunas: Sattva contributes to purity and luminosity. Rajas contributes to movement and transformation. Tamas contributes to heaviness, inertia, and darkness.

**our reality world**: the world of our perception and assumptions.

**self:** one's mistaken sense of *me* as a separate body-mind-ego-personality being; the illusional sense of being a separate entity.

**Self**: spelled with an upper-case S. Our true nature as an individualized unit of the one Reality (God).

- **Self-realization**: direct experience along with accurate knowledge of our essence of being.
- **Soul:** a Self that is identified with mind and a mistaken sense of self.

**ultimate Reality**: The source, sum, and sustainer of all that is. Ultimate Reality has two aspects: a pure essence, and an expressive aspect.

The **pure essence of ultimate Reality** (Existence-Being) is beyond the ability of the mind to conceptualize or describe, but can be experienced in superconscious meditation.

The **expressive aspect of ultimate Reality** has attributes that emanate universes. Other terms referring to this expressive aspect are**: Godhead** -- expressive aspect of God from which the vibrating power (OM) that produces and sustains universes is emanated. **Holy Spirit**: the active, enlivening, vitalizing, and animating aspect of God expressive in creation.

# PERSONAL EVALUATION AND PLANNING FORM

## Life Without Limitations

Use this form and all forms in this program in an honest, reflective manner to assist self-evaluation and to motivate yourself to useful action. Involvement with these forms and projects will make the difference between merely understanding the principles or actually experiencing change and transformation in your life. Because you are dealing with your life in relationship to the Larger Life, you will want to keep these personal and private.

### Respond Honestly to the Following Statements and Directives.

**I possess a good and healthy opinion of myself:**

**If so, you have inner confidence.**

- If not, you need to awaken to an inner awareness of your real nature so that you possess a good and healthy opinion of yourself.

**List here the habits you now have which you would like to change.**

**List here your talents and abilities which you presently use to good advantage, or which could be utilized with training and practice.**

**List the blessings you now enjoy in your life.**

**Do you really want to be free, functional, healthy, and able to live a life without restrictions?**

- If not, why?
- If so, are you willing to pay the price, and do what must be done to allow yourself to live such a life?

**Are you willing to assume personal responsibility for your thoughts, feelings, response to life, decisions, and actions?**

**Are you willing to allow others the freedom to express themselves and to experience their own highest good?**

**Are you willing to be conscious and to know the truth about life, or are there some things you would rather not know?**

As a personal exercise, list here your personal hopes and dreams for yourself and for others and your world. List your goals and your major purposes in life. In this initial project you need not list things in order of priority or importance, just let your thoughts flow, and write what comes to mind that seems useful and important to you.

**My personal hopes and dreams for myself are:**

**My hopes and dreams for others and my world are:**

**My major goals, at the moment, are:**

**My purpose in life, as I see it now, is:**

**Write here your planned schedule for using *The Potential Is Within You* program.**

# THE IDEAL AND THE REALITY

## Life Without Limitations

### *Is a Life Without Limitations Possible?*

***The Nature of the Soul:***

*The soul is a specialized unit of the Larger Life, God.*

*The soul has a destiny in harmony with a Larger Plan.*

*The Natural Inclination of Life:*

*Life's inclination is in the direction of awakening, creative expression, and the fulfillment of purposes.*

*Life's supporting influence (dharma) runs through all of nature.*

*Life supports us when we are open to Life's natural inclination.*

*Man's duty is to prosper in all ways.*

*If the soul is innately endowed with all of the attributes and characteristics of God, why is it that the world is so populated with people who are not expressing freedom?*

*Unknowingness is due to lack of awareness.*

*Some people have the will-to-know but are bound by (temporary) restrictions of the mind, nervous system and physical body.*

*Three characteristics (gunas) run through all of nature, from the Godhead to every aspect of the manifest worlds, including the human mind and body.*

# HOW TO AWAKEN AND EXPRESS THE POTENTIAL WITHIN

## Life Without Limitations

*Every person desires freedom of expression.*
*Every person desires to be happy and free from pain.*
*Every person desires to live, consciously, forever.*

Every person, when healthy and functional, is curious about their world and how and why the universe is as it is. This curiosity leads us to examine the true nature of being and, finally, the true nature of Ultimate Reality.

Man is endowed with a compassionate nature and is inclined to attend to the welfare of his fellow beings and his world.

Expressions of Life are inclined in these directions because this is the natural (innate/inborn) inclination.

All people eventually awaken to the need/desire to examine the nature of life and to discover the truth about it.

Sometimes one awakens because the time is ripe for such awakening.

Others awaken because of need. That is, one may first desire freedom from pain due to restriction. Or, one may be compelled to exercise influence (power) over his personal environment. It does not matter the way one begins his quest, his journey to self-discovery, because eventually he will be led to freedom.

## Are we willing to pay the price?

Instead of thinking in terms of *paying a price*, let us think in terms of letting go of what is not useful in favor of that which is useful and more beneficial.

By emphasizing what is important (essential) and by discarding the non-important, we are able to condense experience, through concentrated endeavor, and greatly accelerate the process of unfoldment and learning. Affirm like this: *I do what I know what I should do to accomplish my purposes, I and I succeed*!

To be inspired to be willing to attend to essentials, contemplate the benefits of purposeful thinking, feeling, and behavior.

Think, feel, and behave like a self-actualized person and you will have the ability, the talents, and the power to be one.

Cultivate ideal attitudes, personal qualities, and skills in relationships. Embody the virtues.

Thinking patterns will be changed beneficially as you assume responsibility for your mental attitude, inner conversations, mental pictures, and verbal expression.

Most personal patterns have been learned or acquired either as a result of imitating other people or as a way to survive and cope. When we function as conscious beings we transcend learned and acquired patterns and express our natural condition. In this way the potential within us is released and finds appropriate expression.

***Six areas of life must be considered if we are to be fulfilled and experience actualization of our potential.***

1. Spiritual health provides perspective and insight for fulfillment at the other levels of life experience.
2. Mental creativity and intellectual capacity are important because mental abilities determine our relationship with the external world. The mental field can be cleansed and purified in a variety of ways.
3. Emotional wellness is essential to peace, serenity, and total health.
4. Physical health and vitality is not only the ideal; it is man's natural condition when all restrictions are cleared.
5. Harmonious interactions and mature relationships with others and the forces in nature contribute to happiness and success in life.
6. Economic freedom and unrestricted movement through the material universe is evidence of one's inner freedom and understanding of the laws of mind and consciousness.

Our values are reflected in our lives by the priorities we establish. Our opinion of what is most important to us is revealed by our words, actions, and relationships. Our environment is a reflection of our own self-image and opinion of ourselves.

One might *almost* master the world and yet fail because of spiritual impoverishment.

To be free or to remain a victim of circumstances is a matter of personal choice once we have come to the realization that we do have a choice. We need not ask anyone else for permission to begin our quest for knowledge or to begin to express our innate abilities. Our real and permanent relationship is with Life.

When using the affirmation below be sure to write your name in order to be personally involved and to impress upon your mind that you are sincere in your intent.

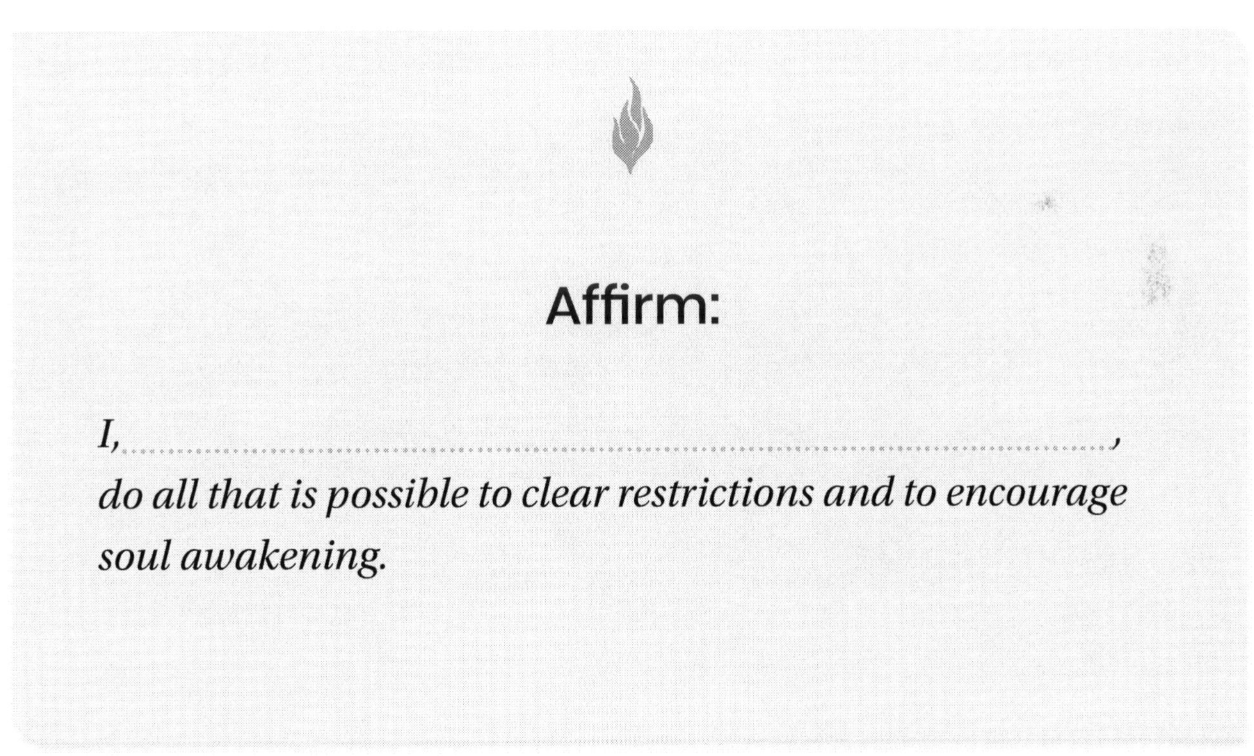

## Affirm:

*I, ............................................................................................,*
*do all that is possible to clear restrictions and to encourage soul awakening.*

# ACTUALIZATION GUIDELINES

## Goal Achievement Plan

**Goal or Final Purpose:**

**Date For Completion/Achievement:**

I complete the purpose or achieve my goal by ..................................................................................................................................................................................................................................................................

**Plans For Completion and/or Achievement:**

**Obstacles Or Restrictions, If Any:**

## SOLUTIONS AND PLANS OF ACTION:

**Expected Benefits as a Result of Actualizing Plans:**

**Affirm:** *I use these plans and experience solutions.*

**Purposes Completed and Goals Achieved:**

**Completed/Achieved:**

Date:

**Completed/Achieved:**

Date:

**Completed/Achieved:**

Date:

*Record short-term gains and achievements as well as long-range ones.*

Use this page for personal notes, ideas, plans of action, or other useful purpose to enable yourself to be consciously involved with your program. You may wish to insert pictures or photos, clippings from published sources, or anything else that would assist your creative process.

# REVIEW

## Life Without Limitations

This review is for your use alone. Do not send it to CSA. By reviewing the material, you afford yourself the opportunity of clearly understanding the essential points and principles. Whenever you read or hear a word or a phrase which is not clearly understood, consult your dictionary or word source. This will improve communication skills and aid memory retention. If you do not know the answers to the below questions, review the material carefully.

*Respond clearly to the following statements and questions:*

**Define the nature of the soul.**

**What is life's natural inclination?**

**Complete the affirmative phrase,** *I do what I know I should do*

**Can we blame lack of education or poor early environmental conditions for our present lot in life if we are not fulfilled?**

**Define the terms *ultimate Reality* and *reality worlds*.**

**Write down any other points you wish to emphasize and remember.**

# SECTION

## 2.

## Self-Realization

# Definitions

**awareness**: The capacity to perceive. Blurred awareness is the cause of erroneous concepts or beliefs resulting from flawed perception of what is observed.

- **modify**: To change the character of something, or to restrict or limit. Awareness is modified by accumulated information, false beliefs, misperceptions, sleep, memories, and fantasies.
- **unmodified awareness**: clear, accurate perception of an object.

**conscious**: state of being aware and observant; capacity to be aware and observant.

**consciousness:** two meanings:

the entity of consciousness itself without an object, which requires no support – often referred to as **pure consciousness**.

1. consciousness as awareness which has an object or supportive relationship, and may be **clear** or may be **modified by** thoughts, memories, delusions (false beliefs), illusions (mistaken perceptions), subliminal impulses, sensory stimulation, emotions, sleep, or mood- or mind-altering substances or behaviors.
2. **Individualized consciousness. Also referred to as Soul-awareness. Soul-consciousness**. Because the soul is a unit of consciousness, we can direct attention inward to experience soul awareness, which is the same as God's awareness. In this way we can determine the nature of God and have faith to continue our spiritual practices. Soul awareness is processed through mind and body. The clearer and more orderly the mind and the more refined the brain and nervous system, the more easily soul consciousness can express.

**mass consciousness**: level of awareness demonstrated by the general population at a given time or era.

**cosmic consciousness:** awareness, usually along with a degree of intuitive apprehension, of the cosmos as a whole, orderly manifestation of cosmic forces.

**superconsciousness**: A clarified **state of awareness** superior to conscious, subconscious, and unconscious states. See *turiya.*

**Consciousness**: with a capital C, denotes God. Also written as **Supreme Consciousness** or **Pure Consciousness.**

**cosmic mind: cosmic mind-substance or universal mind**. The omnipresent mental field of which all individualized minds are an aspect or part. Mind, whether Cosmic or individualized, is comprised of a field of awareness, self-sense, intellect or discerning aspect, and thinking (information processing) aspect. At the level of mind-identification we are in relationship with Cosmic Mind.

**ego**: mistaken sense that one is a separate entity. This mistake is the primary obstacle to Self-realization. When that error in perception is corrected, our awareness can immediately be restored to wholeness.

**egoism:** feeling of, and belief, that one is a separate entity.

- **egotism:** an inflated sense of self-importance.
- **field:** a place in which events occur. A region of space indicated by physical properties such as gravitational or electromagnetic forces.

The expressive aspect of ultimate Reality is a field with attributes that can be emanated as a vibration (OM) that can produce other fields: cosmic individuality, intellect, mind, and causal, astral, and physical fields. Our awareness is a field. Cosmic mind is a field. The Oversoul and primordial nature are fields.

- The pure essence of ultimate Reality is not a field because it is not contained by physical properties.
- **law of mental causation:** Our **mental states** (including our thoughts, desires, intentions, and karmic conditions) interact with Cosmic Mind which is responsive to our mental states. Our mental states are there-by influential in determining our outer experiences.

**levels of mind**: deep unconscious; unconscious; subconscious; conscious.

**mind:** the faculty that stores impressions (memories) of perceptions, and enables thinking, imagination, and reasoning. All minds are units of a **cosmic** or **universal mind** which is inclined to be responsive to mental attitudes, desires, and intentions.

**perception**: awareness or knowledge provided through the five senses or by intellect, reason, intuition, or revelation.

# AFFIRMATIONS PAGE

## I Accept Fulfillment Now

Be alone and meditate until you experience inner peace. Without hurry or anxiety read the following affirmations. Affirm, know, and feel the truth about yourself. Remember, God is expressing as you. You are destined for fulfillment and total understanding.

### I Accept Self-Realization Now

I know I am a specialized unit of God-consciousness, endowed with all of the attributes of the Divine. I practice needed disciplines, study the nature of consciousness, meditate regularly, and surrender ego-sense in order to be consciously aware of my Larger True Self.

### I Accept Mental Clarity and Creativity Now

I regulate my mental pictures, adjust my attitude, see my environment clearly, and fully cooperate with Universal Mind. I set and achieve useful goals in harmony with the highest ideals.

### I Accept Emotional Wellness Now

I come to terms with past experiences, relationships and perceptions. I live appropriately and wisely in the present. I anticipate the near and distant future with serenity, knowing that God is in charge of the world and that grace sustains me, always.

### I Accept Health and Vitality Now

I am established in health-consciousness because I know that true health and vitality extends from the soul level, through mind and into the body. I abide by natural laws relative to nutrition, exercise, rest, and freedom from stress.

### I Accept Loving and Supportive Relationships Now

I know that all people are incarnations of the Divine. I do my part to love and support others and I expect God, through and as other people, to love and support me. In all relationships I serve God and I allow God to serve me.

### I Accept Prosperity and True Fulfillment Now

I know that to *prosper* means to *thrive*, to *flourish*, and to *be successful in useful ways*. I fill real needs. I see human hurts and heal them. I am always open to unplanned good as God meets me at my level of need, on time and in abundance. I share my life and Life's abundance wisely and generously.

I consciously acknowledge this agreement between God and myself and inwardly pledge to do my utmost to abide by my commitment.

“ ”

***There is a Power that runs this universe and we can learn to cooperate with It***

- Roy Eugene Davis

# SELF-REALIZATION

## I Accept Fulfillment Now

### Personal Evaluation and Planning Form

We are now dealing with spiritual values and personal attention to attitudes, thoughts, beliefs, and practices. Because this program is used by persons of various faiths, not all items below may apply to you specifically.

Respond honestly to all of the following statements and questions that are useful in your own personal spiritual life.

**I believe in God.**

- If so, what is your present understanding about God?
- If not, write your reasons for not believing in, or acknowledging, a Supreme Power and Intelligence.

**Prayer is an important part of my daily life.**

- If so, how do you pray?
- If not, why not?
- Should you?
- Do you feel you should?
- If you feel you should, then decide to do so.

**I read the Bible, or the holy scripture of my faith, on a regular schedule.**

- If not, if you are led to do so, begin now to read from selected portions of your own Sacred Book.

**In all that I do, in all relationships, I have thoughts of God in the background of my mind.**

- If not, practice the awareness of the presence of God, always.

**I support the church or spiritual center of my choice with regular attendance and planned financial sharing.**

- Not everyone participates in church or spiritually planned gatherings. This is a matter of inner guidance and choice. But, if you are so connected, are you regular in your participation?
- Do you keep your agreements with yourself and with others on this matter?
- If so, you know it. If not, why not?

**Am I living my ideal life?**

- Would I want for my friends, my family members, and my children to emulate my life as an example?

**If there is need for improvement in this area, write such needs and then implement them according to your inner guidance and strength.**

**What spiritual path or enlightenment tradition am I dedicated to following?**

- If none, write why.
- If you are involved with one, list things you can do to more closely attune yourself to the path of your choice or destiny.

**Am I given to fantasy, or am I realistic about my spiritual studies and understandings?**

- If inclined to fantasy, learn to be more clear and discerning.
- If realistic, continue with love and devotion.

## PERSONAL OBSERVATIONS AND NOTES:

# SELF-REALIZATION

## Enlightenment and the Whole Person

### Enlightenment is Our Natural State

Enlightenment is natural because it is not created. If the state of enlightenment were created, it would not be permanent.

At the center of our being, at the deep soul level, our awareness is pure, clear, unmodified and undistorted.

The real being has always been enlightened, is now fully enlightened, and will always be enlightened.

When one remains conscious and is free from mental and environmental identifications, enlightenment is the natural state.

Enlightenment enables one to clearly comprehend the truth of being, and to contemplate and know the truth about any aspect or manifestation of nature.

Unknowingness is impermanent because every person will, sooner or later, awaken to the truth of being.

Every rational person has an inner awareness of his real and immortal nature. Often this has been *sensed* since infancy, and has been forgotten or obscured because of involvements with externals and the tendency to relate to the opinions and attitudes of others.

Unless it is thwarted, our inner urge to know the truth about life results in a conscious attempt to clear mind and consciousness in order to experience the truth.

Abiding by natural laws and yearning to know the truth about life lead to awakening, unfoldment, and final realization.

## Soul-Level Intelligence Is the True Teacher.

Soul-level intelligence is the intelligence of God because the soul is a specialized unit of God-consciousness.

Inner guidance leads one to search for answers, to strive for mastery, to study the words of enlightened people, and to seek the friendship and association of such people. To resist soul-intelligence is to allow ego to hinder unfoldment and fulfillment.

One may be led to contact a true guru. If not, the inner intelligence of the soul will be the teacher and guide.

## Yearning to Know the Truth Must Be Balanced With Patience.

The guidelines for one on the enlightenment path are simple and universal. They are taught in worldwide traditions and religious and philosophical systems. Regardless of one's faith and religious practice, the central core is the same for everyone because the way to freedom is the same for everyone.

Outer rituals differ according to tradition and custom, but the process of inner awakening and unfoldment is the same. Therefore, all authentic traditions can be respected.

Intentional self-discipline neutralizes destructive and non-useful drives, patterns, and habits, allowing one's real nature to unfold and express.

Careful examination of the nature of consciousness results in perfect understanding from fine levels to gross levels.

Surrender of identification with ego allows the soul to awaken to the realization of its nature as the Larger True Self, God.

The above three guidelines prepare the mind for meditation and contemplation. This is the way of purification.

Without conscious enlightenment man is sense-bound and fails to fulfill his destiny. Living in this world should be relatively easy. After duties and responsibilities are handled, one should then devote the major portion of his time and energy to world upliftment and to the process of assisting others.

We can easily determine our level of awareness. Are we concerned with problems or with solutions? Are we motivated to acquire knowledge or are we content with lack of knowledge? Are we selfish or are we inclined in the direction of cosmic consciousness? Do we take, or do we give to life.

Even an unenlightened person can serve the world by attending to his duties and by living in harmony with the laws of nature. In this way he supports the world and does not cause problems for himself or for others. In this way he prepares himself for eventual spiritual unfoldment.

## Seven Levels of Soul Unfoldment

There are seven levels of soul unfoldment common to all who share the human condition. Seldom is a person established at one level; there are usually characteristics of various levels manifesting in one's life, with one level being the controlling influence—until it, too, is transcended.

***Material consciousness***: When one is fully identified with the physical body and so feels and believes himself to be a body, with a beginning and an end, one is said to be in material consciousness. One at this level of consciousness may be educated, wise in the ways of the world, and performing his duties. One at this level is not to be thought of as being low in consciousness or a threat to his world.

***Initial level of soul awakening:*** At this level one begins to suspect the truth that a more subtle realm lies behind the material one, but is not yet able to comprehend the reality of this realm. Here, he may begin his quest. Or, he may become overly fascinated with phenomena, and lose his way just as surely as one can lose his way in the sense-perceived world if he is not discerning.

***The level where one comprehends the nature of his mind and its relationship with universal mind:*** At this level one is able to comprehend the law of mental causation and is able to participate with universal mind in the setting and achieving of goals and in the matter of cleansing mass consciousness.

The state of true Self-realization: Here the soul becomes aware of its nature as pure consciousness. This is not the stage of final enlightenment but it is a major phase of unfoldment in the direction of freedom or, liberation.

***Cosmic consciousness***: Examining the nature of consciousness with soul intuition one discerns, sees through appearances to that which is so, and forever after lives with perfect understanding. Here, one knows the truth: that the world is a play of lights and shadows, a cosmic drama, a matter of consciousness acting upon itself in infinite variety. This is the experience of true cosmic consciousness.

***God-consciousness***: Transcending any identification with the material realms the soul rests in the awareness of the Godhead, the Oversoul. No longer restricted to the sense of independent existence the soul knows itself as the total Reality.

***The final experience is transcendence***: This is the awareness of Pure Being which can only be experienced , not fully described. It is devoid of characteristics and attributes but it makes possible all outer unfoldments and manifestations.

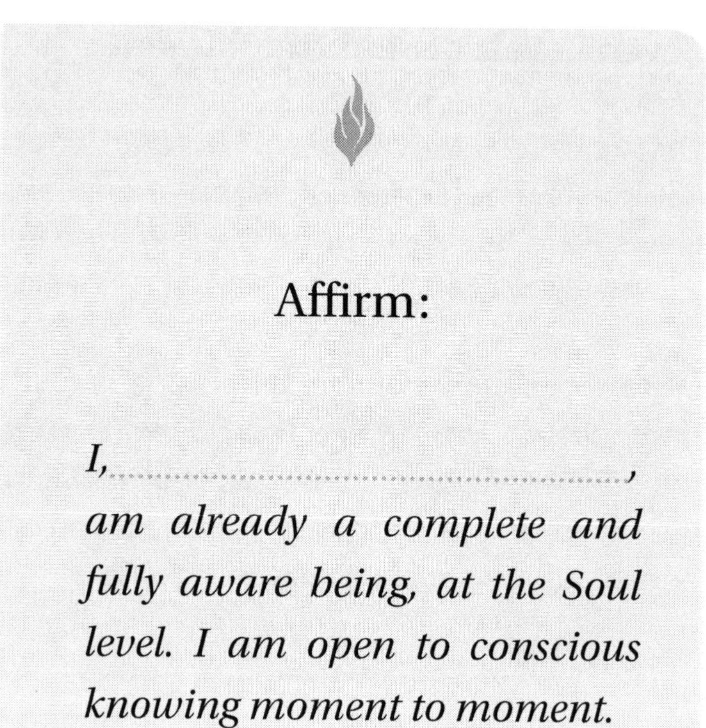


There is no independent universe. There is no individual person. The idea of an independent universe, and the idea of an individual person, are false concepts entertained by one who does not yet know the truth.

The universe is an extension from the source. Since it extends from the source and is sustained by the source, it cannot have independent existence.

The being is a specialized unit of one Larger Consciousness. Since the Oversoul appears as the soul in order to function in relative spheres, there is no individual person. There is one Being; all seemingly independent beings are specialized expressions of the one Being.

Absolute truth cannot be known by the mind. Absolute truth can only be experienced at the soul level. Insight can be acquired through the use of discernment, but experience is of the soul.

The mind is the tool we use, and has no power to know by itself. The discerning aspect of the mind (intelligence) enables us to examine all aspects of a problem and to see through to the solution.

Experience of the truth can be had in a moment of insight even when we are not contemplating. Experience of the truth can also be had during deep meditation when the mental waves have been stilled.

# ACTUALIZATION GUIDELINES

## Goal Achievement Plan

In order to become personally involved with the exercises and processes, it is recommended that you follow the disc Lesson instructions until you are able to practice on your own. The purpose of the written planning forms and the exercises and processes is to afford you the opportunity for inner change and transformation: to translate information into experience.

The process which concludes this lesson is that of resting in the silence, then affirming according to the *I Accept Fulfillment Now* guidelines. Verbal and mental affirmations can greatly contribute to changes in attitude, feeling and thought processes. The key to the ideal use of affirmations is to deeply feel the truth of that which is affirmed. We are not using the power of will to attempt to change patterns. We are gently persuading gradual change to take place. Reconditioning will take place as you use affirmations, but the greater result will be in awakened awareness and clear insight as you find that you become free of the former patterns which restricted.

Write your schedule of planned study and involvement with this program below. Arrange a convenient time when you will have privacy and quiet for this purpose. Remember, it takes at least ten repeated listenings to the spoken instruction before 90% of the material will be retained as accessible memory. Even if you feel you have *heard it before*, do listen over and over again and be open to new insights. You are new every time you examine the material. Now, write your involvement schedule below:

**Goal or Final Purpose:**

**Date For Completion/Achievement:**

I complete the purpose or achieve my goal by ..........................................................

**Plans For Completion and/or Achievement:**

**Obstacles Or Restrictions, If Any:**

## SOLUTIONS AND PLANS OF ACTION:

*I use these plans and experience solutions.*

**Expected Benefits as a Result of Actualizing Plans:**

## PURPOSES COMPLETED AND GOALS ACHIEVED:

**Completed/Achieved:**

Date:

**Completed/Achieved:**

Date:

**Completed/Achieved:**

Date:

*Record short-term gains and achievements as well as long-range ones.*

## GOAL OR FINAL PURPOSE

Use this page for personal notes, ideas, plans of action, or other useful purpose to enable yourself to be consciously involved with your program. You may wish to insert pictures or photos, clippings from published sources, or anything else that would assist your creative process.

# REVIEW

## Self-Realization

*Answer the following questions clearly:*

**Why is enlightenment natural?**

**How long has the real being been enlightened?**

**What leads to awakening, unfoldment, and final realization?**

**Who or what is the true teacher?**

**How many levels of Soul unfoldment are there? From which level do you feel you are primarily functioning?**

**What are the three guidelines which prepare the mind for meditation and contemplation?**

**How can even an unenlightened person serve his world?**

**Why is there no independent universe?**

## Why is there no individual person?

**How can absolute truth be experienced?**

# SECTION

## 3.[a]

## Personal Evaluation and Planning Form

# Definitions

**destiny**: outcomes related to soul-purpose.

**fate:** outcomes related to cause-and-effect.

**law of mind in action**; **mental law of causation**: Because our mind is a portion of universal mind, our mental states impress universal mind, and universal mind expresses accordingly. Understanding the relationship between mental pictures and daily experiences enables us to understand the mental law of causation and to modify our life pattern.

**levels of mind**:

deep unconscious level

- unconscious level
- subconscious
- conscious

**mental field**: mind's magnetic field which contains three influential electrical characteristics which tend to incline the mind to brightness, restlessness, or dullness. Mental field components include:

- **manas, the thinking principle** which enables processing of information.
- **ego,** which enables the sense of separate identity.
- **feeling** principle, which enables desire for fulfillment.
- **intelligence,** which enables discernment between truth and untruth.

**mind**: a creative medium which enables consciousness to relate to the relative spheres.

**universal mind**: omnipresent mind through which omnipresent consciousness relates.

- **individualized mind**: aspect of universal mind through which specialized consciousness (soul) relates.

**our personal world**: reflection of our mental states and of our inner awareness of who we are.

**superconscious level**: soul influence working through the mental field.

# CREATIVE USE OF THE MIND

**Respond honestly to the following statements:**

**I am conscious and alert, and use my faculties of discrimination (my intelligence) to discern the truth of any situation.**

**I avail myself of information if needed to improve function.**

**I understand the relationship between my mind and the larger mind (universal mind).**

**I make decisions easily.**

**I make a conscious effort to regulate my interior conversations and verbal comments.**

**My environment is well-ordered and reflects my well-ordered thoughts.**

**I take full responsibility for my mental attitude, interior conversations, mental pictures, and actions.**

**I am open to new and useful ideas.**

**When faced with a problem I practice possibility thinking.**

**I am willing to learn from others who are successful and who have demonstrated self-actualization and spiritual understanding in their own lives.**

**I am willing to devote time and attention to learning new and better ways to accomplish my purposes and achieve my goals.**

**When faced with a challenge I see it as an opportunity to apply my creative mental abilities.**

**I understand that I am a spiritual being living in a spiritual world; this awareness allows me to function accordingly and to see demonstrated results in my life and my world.**

# CREATIVE USE OF THE MIND

Use this page to practice writing useful affirmations which can be used during the day to regulate mental states, correct thinking patterns, and adjust behavior. Always affirm in the present tense; that is, affirm now that you are the kind of person you have long desired to be, and that you are possessed of all natural abilities and talents. Be the person you are meant to be: think the thoughts you were meant to think, feel the feelings which contribute to health and success, relate and function as a competent self-actualized, spiritually aware person from this moment forward. A sample affirmation follows:

*I am a conscious and intelligent person. I make wise use of my mental abilities, I plan intelligently, I begin and complete my planned programs of action, and in all ways I am fulfilled and successful.*

*Note*: Use any affirmative statement made on these evaluation forms as a personal affirmation. If the statement is not true of you, write an affirmation beneath it which would assist you to change to conform to the ideal.

***Always Be Open to Your Unplanned Good!***

# CREATIVE USE OF THE MIND

## Mind: What It Is & How It Works

### Mind:

Mind is a creative medium which enables consciousness to relate to the relative spheres. Universal mind is omnipresent mind through which omnipresent consciousness relates, and individualized mind is that through which specialized consciousness (soul) relates.

Universal mind is omnipresent, present everywhere. All of the characteristics of universal mind are also innate (indwelling) to specialized mind.

The mental field is a magnetic field and contains three electrical characteristics which tend to influence it. Depending upon the dominant electrical characteristic, the mind is inclined to brightness, restlessness, or inertia, dullness.

Use of the mind can lead to enlightenment and fulfillment, or it can lead to further bondage and limitation. Wise use of the mind results in freedom; unwise use of the mind results in restriction.

### Components of Mind:

There are four basic aspects which make up the mental field.

The thinking principle (manas, from the Sanskrit) is the aspect of the mind most commonly considered. This aspect enables us to examine, compare, compute, make decisions, and arrive at possible solutions to problems. We can also make choices, set goals, and determine to be responsible for how we use the mind and how we behave and relate.

Ego is the false sense of separate existence. This aspect gives rise to the awareness one has of "I" as being apart from the source. The real being is really cosmic, both omnipresent and specialized. All drives to satisfy ego needs are likely to lead to further confusion.

***The feeling principle*** enables us to desire, fulfill desires, and experience a degree of satisfaction. Blind desire leads to addictions and limitation. Desire guided by reason enables us to achieve goals and fulfill our destiny.

***The aspect of intelligence*** enables us to discern, to see clearly the truth in contrast to that which is not truth.

## Levels of the Mind:

The mind is one field in which all mental functions occur; we postulate differing spheres, or levels, for the purpose of convenience in understanding mental processes.

***Deep unconscious level***: The deep unconscious level of mind is not accessible to most people. Here reside all of the dormant urges, desires, and inclinations. Here also reside memories long forgotten.

***Unconscious level***: This level of mind contains impressions which influence us even if we do not know of their existence.

***Subconscious level***: This level of mind accepts impressions, files and relates them, stores memory, responds to suggestions, and is the responsive level of the mind.

***Conscious level*:** This level of mind is used during wakefulness, although there are degrees of awareness at all levels of mind.

***The Superconscious level of mind*** is that level which remains conscious and clear, always, and is not influenced by the other levels. The more superconscious influences act upon the full range of the mental field, the greater is the experience of mind-cleansing and transformation. Superconscious influence is really soul-influence working through the mental field.

## Modifications of the Mind:

Relative clarity while handling conditionings and patterns is the normal experience of functional people who are seeking greater understanding. However, while working through the mental field one may relate to one or more modifications of the mind, depending upon clarity of perception, and intent in the quest for knowledge and freedom.

## Modifications include:

**Perceptual errors in addition to the accurate perceptions**: Errors in perception may result in illusion. Failing to see what is so results in lack of accurate communication with the environment. That is, one may assume that what is perceived is accurate, and then live in that illusion.

**Fantasy**: Imaginings. Living in a mental condition of mind-created fantasy is the cause of hallucination. This is sometimes due to our unwillingness to confront life, and it is sometimes due to an imbalance in body chemistry that affects the brain, or to some disorder of the nervous system.

**Memory**: A functional person should have easy access to memory impressions. However, to be caught in the habit of dwelling on memories instead of the present and future is an avoidance of responsible behavior.

**Sleep**: Sleep is common to almost all creatures, including man. During sleep we experience rest and rejuvenation, and the mind and nervous system release stress. For a conscious person the hours of sleep can be used productively.

**Unconscious impulses**: Tendencies from deeper layers of mind can also invade the subconscious and conscious levels, resulting in compulsions, drives, and destructive and non-useful behavior. These tendencies can be resisted, restrained, and cleansed from the mental field with conscious practice and the experience of deep meditation.

## Mind: How to Use It:

The first step in the direction of using the mind creatively and wisely is to make a decision to be responsible for our mental attitudes, thought patterns, interior conversations, mental pictures, and verbal conversations.

We have the power of choice regarding the mental attitudes we assume and maintain day to day and moment to moment.

Though thought patterns often seem to have "life" of their own, they can be regulated with practice and intention.

We all carry on inner conversations. Becoming aware of these conversations, and either stopping them by purposely redirecting attention or regulating them, gives us mastery.

The mental pictures we entertain tend to condition the subconscious level of mind. Firm mental pictures tend to eventually externalize as experiences and relationships. Understanding the relationship between mental pictures and daily experiences enables us to understand the mental law of causation and to modify our life pattern.

When we consciously regulate our conversations and the verbal statements that we make, we find that we have a powerful tool with which to regulate deeper mental processes.

We learn to cooperate intentionally with universal mind when we become responsible for our mental states and states of consciousness. Our personal *world* is a reflection of our mental states and of our inner awareness of who we are.

Because our mind is a portion of universal mind, our mental states impress universal mind, and universal mind expresses accordingly. This is the law of mind in action.

Our awareness of being, our awareness of who we are as, a spiritual entity, determines our thoughts and attitudes. When we are fully aware of who we are, we naturally see ideal situations and relationships and we easily see the possibility of doing whatever it is we are inclined to do. When we function from the level of being we do not have to try to succeed, we are automatically successful.

Unless mental attitude is altered and unless our awareness of who we are is changed, we will continue through life as we have been.

The mental law of causation is impersonal: it will respond to anyone who will learn of it and use it. Wise use of the law results in fulfillment and happiness for a person and for all with whom he relates. Unwise use of the law causes conflict, injury to self and others, and leads to future difficulties.

We can use the law of mental causation wisely or we can use it unwisely, and the results will be according to how we use it.

We are wise to use the law of mental causation intentionally and wisely because this is a natural ability that we have and we were meant to use it. As long as one thinks in terms of benefits, for oneself and all concerned, one will be inclined to make wise use of the law.

We are now experiencing the results of past thoughts, desires, and expectations. This is fate: this is the result of past causes. Fate can be changed when we are willing to introduce into the mental field new causes, new thoughts, new worthwhile desires, and altruistic expectations.

We are driven to fulfill our soul-purpose. This is destiny. Destiny is sometimes modified by fate but destiny will prevail, sooner or later. Therefore, it is useful for us to pray, to contemplate, to be open to inner guidance in order to coordinate the law of mental causation with our own soul destiny.

An urge to do or to experience can be the result of ego-drive, deeper-mind inclinations, or the urge of the soul to fulfill destiny. Through calm self-analysis we can learn to discern the difference between various urges, and select the ones which lead to the fulfillment of soul destiny.

The three keys to certain success in the use of the law of mental causation are: idealize, believe, and achieve. This is the way to certain fulfillment regardless of the reasonable goal.

To idealize is to picture, to plan, to hope for a final useful result. We move forward into our mental pictures, into what we feel we deserve to experience. We may desire an experience but if we do not feel worthy of it, we will not be able to accept it as our personal right.

To believe that we are worthy of any useful experience and to believe in its *reality* attracts that experience and all that is required for it to manifest.

When we fully experience the reality of our desires, we have achieved. Our goals are experienced and we move on to new useful goals.

The setting and the achieving of goals is but an experience; the ideal is to be fulfilled so that goal achievement is routine and automatic. To "live" to achieve a goal is limitation; to be fulfilled and to experience easy goal achievement as a process of enlightened living is the ideal. When all useful goals are achieved, when destiny has been fulfilled, the soul transcends the need for relative relationships.

How we use our time and energy is an indication of how we feel about ourselves and reveals our private thoughts about our relationship to God. God's inclination is in the direction of awakening, unfoldment, and the completion of purposes. If we waste our time and energy we are wandering through time and space without purpose. If we invest our time and energy we are planning with purpose.

In this world we have time and we have energy to expend. How do we use our time and how do we direct our available energy? By examining our motives, we can easily arrive at an answer. Time can be managed and energy can be transformed. The energy we expend can result in useful happenings if we are so directed. Energy not used can be returned to the inner areas of life, and there be transmuted into subtle and fine energies for higher purposes.

Even enlightened men and women invest time and energy in the direction of a final purpose. They do this because they are inwardly aware of a larger plan for the world process. They see themselves as but individualized units of the process.

Ego-satisfaction leads but to the grave; soul-fulfillment results in enlightenment. Physical death (transition to another sphere) is not the end, but believing the process to be final results in more "lessons" to be learned by the soul. The final lesson is to awaken and to be fully conscious.

Listening to inner soul guidance and then following through with an intelligently-directed plan of action is the way of wisdom for all of us, for you and for me.

Deep within, each person knows the difference between what is useful and what is not useful, what is correct and what is not correct relative to the overall good. We are not here talking about those who are bound by neurotic or psychotic influences.

To set and achieve goals, write a plan of action to clarify thinking, to picture the outcome, and to make a definite decision.

Since our mind is observed and used by us, the mind is our creative tool. Mind has no power in itself. The seeming power of mind is soul-power which flows through the mental field.

The mind has no will of its own. There are tendencies and inclinations but these are the effects of prior conditioning. These conditionings can be neutralized.

Even we have no personal power. Whatever power is used is the power of God, our Larger True Self. The more we become free from ego-drive, the greater is our success and permanent fulfillment.

The mind can be educated through intentional practice. Unwanted patterns can be removed and we can then express through the mind without restriction. Here is an exercise for daily practice: Rest in the stillness until the mental patterns become dormant.

Acknowledge the truth about yourself: *Consciousness is what I am.*

Acknowledge that there is but one mind. Your mind is a portion of the one mind. You, therefore, have access to the total field of mind and you can work in harmony with it.

Be established in the awareness of this truth. Be firmly anchored in this realization. Feel good about it as you accept it fully. Function consciously in partnership with the one mind.

## Affirm:

*I, ......................................................................................,*
*make wise use of my mental abilities and work in harmony with universal mind.*

## ACTUALIZATION GUIDELINES

To reinforce your intentions to order your thoughts and to work in harmony with universal mind, consider the following, and follow through with those plans which are needed for your success.

- Read whatever supportive material you require to keep yourself motivated and inspired.
- Arrange your personal environment to agree with your plans for change, if needed, and to reflect your new attitude about yourself and your role in life. Remove clutter from your environment and arrange for yourself an orderly and efficient working space.
- Plan to make efficient use of your time and energy.
- When with other people be sure to regulate your conversation so that it reflects a positive and constructive purpose. Do not allow others to confuse you or cause you to assume a negative outlook on life.
- Use positive affirmations daily, whenever needed, to maintain the ideal mental attitude.
- Set useful short-term and long-term goals. Now. Write them clearly and select dates for completion.
- Short-term goals enable you to experience accomplishment right away, and this will boost self-confidence. These goals can be planned so they are easy to reach. Success motivates us to more and greater success.
- Reward yourself when you achieve your goals. Take your family or a friend to dinner, make wanted purchases, begin to experience the benefits of goal achievement.
- Be sure to be involved with a total program because every area of life influences all other areas. See to meditation, study, goal achievement, creative imagination, emotional wellness, health and vitality, supportive relationships, and true prosperous living. Do not neglect any area of life. Be a total person. Be a fully and radiantly alive self-actualized, spiritually aware person!
- If need be, visit places which inspire and motivate you, and read magazines and literature which give you ideas and assist you to move into the mental attitude and the state of consciousness you want to permanently experience in your life.

## GOAL ACHIEVEMENT PLAN

**Goal or Final Purpose:**

**Date For Completion/Achievement:**

I complete the purpose or achieve my goal by ______________________.

**Plans For Completion and/or Achievement:**

**Obstacles Or Restrictions, If Any:**

## SOLUTIONS AND PLANS OF ACTION:

*I use these plans and experience solutions.*

**Expected Benefits as a Result of Actualizing Plans:**

## PURPOSES COMPLETED AND GOALS ACHIEVED:

**Completed/Achieved:**

Date:

**Completed/Achieved:**

Date:

**Completed/Achieved:**

Date:

*Record short-term gains and achievements as well as long-range ones.*

## GOAL OR FINAL PURPOSE

Use this page for personal notes, ideas, plans of action or other useful purpose to enable you to be consciously involved with your program. You may wish to insert pictures or photos, clippings from published sources, or anything else that would assist your creative process.

# REVIEW

## Creative Use of the Mind

*Answer the following questions clearly:*

**Explain the difference between our mind and universal mind.**

**What are the four basic aspects of the mental field?**

**Describe the superconscious level of mind.**

**What is the first step to be taken if one is to use the mind creatively and wisely?**

**Do we have a choice about what our mental attitude will be?**

**What powerful tool do we have at our disposal for the regulating of deeper mental processes?**

**Is the law of mental causation personal or impersonal?**

**What are the three keys to certain success in the use of the law of mental causation?**

**Complete:**

*Time can be managed and* ..................................................................................................................................................... .

**Is there any power in mind?**

# SECTION

## 3.b

## Personal Evaluation and Planning Form

# CREATIVE IMAGINATION

*Respond honestly to the following statements and questions:*

**I am open to heretofore undreamed-of possibilities.**

**I enjoy reading inspirational books and publications.**

**I enjoy hearing of the success stories others share.**

**Can you accept the teaching that the "world is plastic and fluid" and takes the mental impress of what we think and believe?**

**What wonderful things would you do, and what would you experience, if you knew that failure were impossible?**

**Do you ever feel that you were destined to fail?**

- Why?

**Do you feel that you are often the effect of past causes which cannot be changed?**

- If so, write these presumed causes.

**Are you willing to release present relationships if this is necessary in order for your dreams to manifest?**

**Do you resist change of any kind?**

**How many publications do you read which relate to your special sphere of interest?**

- List them.

**Are you afraid of success?**

- List the reasons if this applies.

**Are you self-centered, or do you take in a larger sphere of responsibility?**

**How big is your world?**

**List some of the people who have greatly influenced you.**

- Why?

**Use the space here for any other notes to yourself which might be useful:**

# CREATIVE IMAGINATION: YOUR GIFT AND HOW TO USE IT

## See Your Dreams Come True

### Man Possesses the Gift of Creative Imagination.

Everyone has the gift of imagination. Some can picture more vividly than others but all can do it. Recall a recent time when you enjoyed an unusual meal and describe it. As you recall the occasion you will be using mental imagery.

By engaging in possibility-thinking and intentional acts of creative imagination we can see, in the mind's eye, new or different desirable states of consciousness or personal experiences and relationships. According to the law of mental causation, when we firmly hold to mental pictures which conform to our heart's desire, we can attract all of the essentials required to embody that desire. Or, because of a new state of consciousness and a new mental attitude, we can see that which we desire to be already in existence and then accept it as ours.

### The Technique:

The technique is simple to understand and easy to use. Self-actualized persons use the method automatically. First, be clear about your goal or goals. Decide if you really want what you affirm. Be willing to release all attitudes and mental-emotional characteristics which are not compatible with the ideal you envision.

Sit or recline in a quiet place and become fully relaxed. Allow the mind to become clear, and experience yourself as consciousness alone.

On the inner screen of your mind, picture yourself in a situation or relationship which would confirm that your desire is already fulfilled, your goal already achieved.

At this stage do not think of how or of any of the steps needed to experience fulfillment and achievement. Just picture yourself in the final situation.

Feel this to be true with all of the tones of reality, with taste, touch, smell, sight, hearing. Live in the experience of the wish fulfilled. Inwardly know and feel, *It is done. How wonderful*! Feel how you would feel if it were already outwardly true, because it is already true in your imagination.

Either go to sleep, or sink more deeply into the feeling and inner experience until it is permanent in mind and consciousness.

## After Practicing:

Once you are established in the feeling of accomplishment, your mental attitude will be changed, your self-opinion will be altered, and creative ideas will surface in the mind. Write any useful ideas and begin a planned program of involvement which will enable you to see your desire fulfilled. Use the forms provided with this program or use other sheets of paper.

While planning and working in the direction of goal achievement, be sure to maintain the feeling and inner knowing that the goal is already as good as achieved. Whenever you waver, whenever your faith falters, again practice the technique of creative imagination. If we can firmly establish ourselves in the feeling and knowing, only one session is needed for the practice of the technique.

Tell no one about your inner work or about your goals unless others are part of your personal project. Be steady in faith because this will seemingly work miracles. "Faith is the substance of things hoped for, the evidence of things unseen."

Some desires are almost instantly realized while others take time because events and circumstances have to come together. Be patient while events and circumstances are coming together. Remember, you are already established, in mind and consciousness, in the wish fulfilled. Your desires are on the way to being realized, unless deeper desires and needs are stronger and more important. Sometimes we know, at the soul level, what is really best for us even though this is not known at the conscious mind level. When practicing the technique of creative imagination, you might add the thought: *I am open to experiencing* that which I now envision, or something better for me, something more useful in the long run.

If action is required, do all you can to assist the creative process and then wait for the unfoldment.

Be open to the possibility of unplanned good fortune. Life has ways of providing for you what you have not yet thought about. Learn to see opportunities at every hand, learn to be open to nourishment and support however life meets you at your level of need and acceptance.

Remove from your life and from your environment anything and everything that does not conform to the ideal you envision for yourself.

Think, feel, and act as though failure were impossible.

It is possible to imagine and plan for several goals at once. Many projects will be inter-related. Be sure to plan short-term and long-term projects. The more you succeed the greater will be your self-confidence, and the greater will be your ability to function.

When practicing the technique of creative imagination, if you find it difficult at first to vividly picture a scene or situation which conforms to your ideal, do this: In your mind's eye, think of a trusted friend in whom you have the utmost confidence. Have your friend tell you how happy they are to see you now as a fulfilled and successful person. Respond with thanks, just as you would were your friend to actually stand before you and speak these words. Feel fulfilled and happy as confirmation that your goal has been achieved and your wishes fulfilled.

This process can be used to set and reach goals, to assist others in need of help, and to change our own image of ourselves. By picturing ourselves as we want to be, as we can be, as we deserve to be, we call forth all of the characteristics from within ourselves and we actually become the embodiment of the person we were destined to be.

Creative imagination awakens awareness and enables us to actualize the potential within. The more we use creative imagination effectively, the more capable we become and the easier the process works for us.

Creative imagination is the method used by many people to induce subtle changes on mental, emotional, and physical levels, resulting in healing on all levels. Life's natural inclination is in the direction of health and function. When obstructions to this inclination are removed, health and function are automatic.

Nourish the mind with motivational thoughts, inspirational reading, and with accomplishment. Train yourself to think constructively and clearly. Read material for motivation and inspiration. Every time we succeed, we become stronger and more proficient. This is the way to self-actualization and spiritual growth.

Now, practice the technique of creative imagination.

## Affirm:

*I, ........................................................................................................,*
*practice the technique of creative imagination until I am skilled in the use of it.*

# ACTUALIZATION GUIDELINES

Study the technique of creative imagination until you understand the process completely. This process has been called *the success method that never fails.* With it, you have the key to altering your point of view, your mental attitude, and the way you look at life. With it, you can open doors, see new opportunities, and mobilize your resources and energies in a constructive manner. With it, you can learn to consciously relate to an ever-changing world with understanding.

Practice the process daily in order to become proficient and successful in its use.

Constantly be open to your unplanned good. Life is seeking to express through and around you in full measure. Learn to flow with life.

A useful time to practice is as you go to sleep at night. Another useful time is early morning, when you have started to awaken but are still in a reverie state of consciousness. At this time you are inwardly free to let your imagination soar in a creative and directed manner.

Before going to sleep, remind yourself to be conscious when you dream. Before long, you will find that you are conscious while in the midst of an ongoing dream experience. Remember how this felt when you awaken, and compare the dream state with the waking state. You will soon see similar patterns and you will see that your waking world is very much like the dream world in that you can handle yourself in relationship to situations and circumstances with objectivity and mastery. Your outer world does reflect your expectation of it.

Just as your dreams take place in your mind, your waking relationships take place in your own mental spaces. You can learn to see in your waking world what you choose to see. You can learn to call forth relationships, resources, all that is required for your fulfillment, from the world about you. This is the law of attraction. We attract to ourselves what we expect and feel worthy of having as part of our experience.

Once you are firmly convinced that you are on the right track for yourself, do not give up. Know that what you are seeking is also seeking you. Refuse to accept limitation or defeat. Live by faith in the face of seeming obstacles, and do your part to be the person you must be to handle the responsibilities you feel led to handle.

If you meditate before using the technique of creative imagination, use the technique just after meditation while you are still resting in the relaxed state of awareness, the state of awareness from which you can believe that all things are possible.

# PERSONAL EVALUATION AND PLANNING FORM

As an exercise in imagination let your mind be open as you write all of the things you would like to do and experience in this present life-cycle. Be as bold and as daring as you like. Write as you have the idea or goal; later, you can list some of the things in order of importance or priority.

***All Things Are Possible.***

Now that you have listed the things you would like to do and experience in this life-cycle, go over the list and write some of the projects in order of importance or personal priority.

# GOAL ACHIEVEMENT PLAN

**Goal or Final Purpose:**

**Date For Completion/Achievement:**

I complete the purpose or achieve my goal by ______.

**Plans For Completion and/or Achievement:**

**Obstacles Or Restrictions, If Any:**

# SOLUTIONS AND PLANS OF ACTION:

*I use these plans and experience solutions.*

**Expected Benefits as a Result of Actualizing Plans:**

**Purposes Completed and Goals Achieved:**

**Completed/Achieved:**

Date:

**Completed/Achieved:**

Date:

**Completed/Achieved:**

Date:

*Record short-term gains and achievements as well as long-range ones.*

# GOAL OR FINAL PURPOSE

Use this page for personal notes, ideas, plans of action. or other useful purpose to enable yourself to be consciously involved with your program. You may wish to insert pictures or photos, clippings from published sources, or anything else that would assist your creative process.

## REVIEW

### Creative Imagination

*Answer the following questions clearly:*

**Does everyone possess the gift of creative imagination?**

**List the four stages in the practice of the technique.**

**Is it possible to plan several goals at once?**

**If you find it difficult to envision, while practicing the technique, what alternative method can you use?**

After you have experimented with the technique, if you have any areas in which you require improvement, go over the lesson for assistance.

# SECTION

## 4.[a]

## Personal Evaluation and Planning Form

# THE SCIENCE OF MEDITATION

## I Am Interested in Meditating Because:

*I am new to the concept of meditation.*
*I already meditate successfully.*

**I experience obstacles to meditation, such as:**

I realize that various meditation methods are useful to different people because individuals vary in temperament and capacity.

**When I meditate, I experience:**

I am willing to experience useful change and inner transformation as a result of correct meditation experience.

Use the rest of this page and the reverse for any personal notes to yourself for the purpose of self-evaluation and planning.

# THE SCIENCE OF MEDITATION

## The Process, Methods, and Techniques

### What is Meditation?

- Meditation is the process by which we are able to relax the body, clear the mental field and experience our nature as pure being.
- Correct meditation practices result in relaxation of the body, de-stressing of the nervous system and clearing of the mental field as thought processes become dormant.
- Meditation is not auto-conditioning or self-hypnosis.
- Meditation is not a mental exercise. It is the process of flowing attention back to the source of life within.

### Why Should One Meditate?

- Meditation affords one the opportunity of conscious rest and the occasion to experience clear undisturbed awareness.
- Deep meditation is more refreshing than ordinary sleep.
- During meditation the involuntary nervous system is given the opportunity to rest.
- Advanced meditators experience an awakening of vital forces which actually neutralize the decay process of the body.
- Meditation results in superconscious forces invading the mental field. These forces resist, restrain and, finally, neutralize destructive drives and tendencies in the mental field.
- Meditation awakens intuition, increases energy flow, sharpens intellectual abilities and results in an aware ness of harmony with life.

- As a result of resting in the experience of being, we are inclined to find that constructive patterns emerge and we are more inclined to live a natural life.
- Meditation affords the mind the opportunity to experience a degree of refined pleasure which is superior to the pleasure experience resulting from any other cause. This enables one to more easily renounce harmful addictions.
- Meditation prepares us for contemplation so that we can examine the true meaning of life and experience insight.

## What Happens When We Meditate?

Careful examination of meditators, while meditating, indicate specific changes which can be monitored. These changes and conditions are unique to the meditative experience and are not found, in combination, during any other state of human consciousness.

- The physical body experiences deep relaxation.
- Body temperature is lowered.
- The breathing pattern slows and becomes finer.
- Heart action slows down.
- Blood pressure, if high, tends to lower in the direction of normal and remains lower as long as meditation is practiced on a regular schedule.
- While meditating, the body consumes less oxygen and pro duces less carbon dioxide.
- Blood specimens indicate a reduced presence of lactic acid, proving lowered stress in body systems.
- Brain wave patterns tend to be synchronized and indicate orderly functioning of the brain and nervous system.

When one is meditating correctly the mental field becomes clear as patterns become dormant. The mind is not rendered blank and one does not become unconscious. The mind remains clear and the person remains fully alert and conscious.

## Who Should Meditate?

Since healthful benefits are the natural result of meditation, all people should meditate in order to experience conscious rest and to allow the awakening of soul potential.

- Any person, in any walk of life, can only benefit from regular meditation practice.

Children can be taught to meditate and learn easily. Tests indicate that children who meditate are calmer, experience improvement in concentration and memory, get along better with parents and peers and establish superior work habits.

- Meditation should be practiced on a regular schedule.
- To meditate in a group can also be useful.

## How Does One Meditate?

The process is easy to learn. There are many methods and techniques to meet various personal needs. Let's deal with a very simple process first. Even persons who have been meditating for a while and who are not experiencing benefits, should return to the practice- of this basic process as here described.

- Sit quietly in a place where you will not be disturbed.Allowatleast20to30minutesfor the process.
- Sit upright, with spine straight and head erect. Close your eyes and look upward in the direction of the space between the eyebrows. This will tend to "lift" attention and body forces upward, away from the senses.
- Allow the body to breathe naturally. Do not regulate the breathing process. Feel the body breathe and observe the process.
- Let the process continue. With inhalation, feel the process, with exhalation, feel the process and mentally listen to a meaningless sound, such as the word "one". The reason for this is to afford the attention a point of focus. Note that we are not counting down into a deeper level of mind. We are merely feeling the breathing pattern and listening to the sound of a meaningless word with out-breathing. The reason for listening to the sound of a meaningless word is that a word with meaning would prompt thinking.
- Continue this process for at least 20 minutes to allow your self the opportunity to relax and derive benefit.
- Emerge from your practice session and become creatively involved with your projects and relationships.

Practice the above process twice a day without any anxiety for results and without overly examining the process. After a few weeks reflect a bit and notice any changes in attitude, feelings and behavior. You see, the process is very simple and easy to practice.

There are some obstacles to meditation practice and these can be eradicated. Do not struggle with the process, just experience it.

One may be inclined to go to sleep while meditating. This may be the conditioned response to relaxation. Keeping the gaze upward and the attention upward, while sitting upright, will help you to avoid sleep.

One may have the inclination to daydream, to wander along a stream of thoughts, or to call up memories of prior experiences. Avoid these inclinations by remaining attentive to the breathing pattern and the inner sound.

You will want to avoid any tendency to become overly fascinated with mental pictures or any inner perception. What ever is perceived, renounce it and let it go. The ideal experience is conscious clear awareness.

Unwanted body movement may disturb concentration. There fore, sit in a comfortable position and do not move while meditating. With practice this will be quite natural to do.

There is nothing to fear as a result of meditation practice. When you meditate correctly you are but returning consciously to the source of life within the body. This results in health, improved function and an enhancement of life-appreciation. Have nothing to do with others who try to tell you of dangers or who insist that there is a possibility of your being influenced by others when you are quiet. You are not passive when you meditate correctly, you are conscious and fully alert.

What about prayer? Is meditation the same as contemplation? These are questions which are often asked by meditators and by those who are interested in meditation. Prayer is our mental or verbal inter action with God, our Larger True Self. We can pray however we are inclined or however we feel best about the process. We can pray until the mind is clear and the feelings settled, then rest in the stillness and experience spontaneous meditation. Many people, who meditate for the relaxation benefits do not pray as part of the exercise. If you are more devotional you will be inclined to pray. Prayer can be a useful part of the total meditation program.

Contemplation means to direct attention to an area of life for which insight is desired. One might contemplate a solution for a problem, after meditating. One might examine some aspect of philosophy, a verse of scripture, the meaning of life, man's relationship with God, or whatever is meaningful at the moment. Contemplation is always best practiced after meditation because then the mind is more clear and the faculties of intelligence and intuition are unveiled.

The great value of regular meditation practice is that it enables us to enter into a conscious and harmonious relationship with life. Rest and activity...rest and activity ...is the way of nature. To sleep and then to awaken is common to all people. A superior mode of resting is to rest consciously in the awareness of pure being during meditation.

***Practice meditation.***

## Affirm:

*I,........................................................................................................,*
*will establish a regular routine of meditation practice to suit my needs.*

# GOAL ACHIEVEMENT PLAN

**Goal or Final Purpose:**

**Date For Completion/Achievement:**

I complete the purpose or achieve my goal by ................................................................................

**Plans For Completion and/or Achievement:**

**Obstacles Or Restrictions, If Any:**

# SOLUTIONS AND PLANS OF ACTION:

*I will use these plans and experience solutions.*

**Expected Benefits as a Result of Actualizing Plans**

**Purposes Completed and Goals Achieved:**

**Completed/Achieved:**

Date:

**Completed/Achieved:**

Date:

**Completed/Achieved:**

Date:

*Record short-term gains and achievements as well as long-range ones.*

Use this page for personal notes, ideas, plans of action or for whatever useful purpose to enable you to be consciously involved with your program. You may wish to insert pictures or photos, clippings from published sources ,anything to assist the creative process.

# REVIEW

## The Science of Meditation

**What is meditation?**

**Is meditation the same as auto-conditioning or self-hypnosis?**

- If not, why not?

**List a few reasons why a person should meditate.**

**List a few things that happen when one meditates correctly.**

**List a few possible obstacles to meditation and their correction.**

**What does it mean to contemplate?**

**Should meditation be practiced on a regular schedule?**

- Why?

# SECTION

## 4.b

## The Science of Meditation

# CREATIVE AND DYNAMIC PRACTICE

The major portion of this session is the actual practice of meditation in a creative and dynamic manner. Use the recorded program as often as needed until you can practice on your own. Use it anytime for reinforcement. Once you are established in a meditation routine you will find that the inner awareness of you knows how to meditate. Since this is an involvement session, this page will also be your opportunity to participate by writing a schedule for meditation which suits your needs.

***When you plan to meditate:*** ........................................

***How often you plan to meditate:*** ........................................

***Alone or with another:*** ........................................

Even if a meditation partner cannot join you, be sure to keep to your regular schedule. Regularity will enable you to neutralize any subconscious resistance to the process and will afford you the opportunity to experience benefits which will, in turn, inspire you to continue in a creative manner.

Meditation for relaxation and stress-management: If you are in need of reducing stress from the systems of the body then practice the method of observing/feeling the breathing pattern for at least 20 minutes two times a day.

Deeper meditation practice: Allow the process to continue until you experience inner release and an awareness of fulfillment. Pray before and after meditation, feel attuned to the reality of God. After meditation use any affirmative program you find useful to stabilize you in clear awareness. Think well of the world and love and bless others and your world.

Do not become fascinated with mental pictures while meditating. Do not become anxious to see an inner light or to hear sounds. The most beneficial experience will be that of peace, serenity and an awareness of attunement with life. Everything else will unfold in perfect proportion for you, in due course of time.

## GOAL ACHIEVEMENT PLAN

### Goal or Final Purpose

**Date For Completion/Achievement:**

I complete the purpose or achieve my goal by ............................................................................................................................................................................ .

**Plans For Completion and/or Achievement:**

**Obstacles Or Restrictions, If Any:**

# SOLUTIONS AND PLANS OF ACTION:

*I will use these plans and experience solutions.*

**Expected Benefits as a Result of Actualizing Plans:**

## PURPOSES COMPLETED AND GOALS ACHIEVED:

**Completed/Achieved:**

Date:

**Completed/Achieved:**

Date:

**Completed/Achieved:**

Date:

*Record short-term gains and achievements as well as long-range ones.*

## GOAL OR FINAL PURPOSE

Use this page for personal notes, ideas, plans of action or for whatever useful purpose to enable you to be consciously involved with your program. You may wish to insert pictures or photos, clippings from published sources anything to assist the creative process.

# SECTION

## 5.a

## Keys to Emotional Wellness

# PERSONAL EVALUATION AND PLANNING FORM

***Respond honestly to the following statements:***

**I never feel frustrated.**

- If you do sometimes, explain, and write suggestions for avoiding frustration.

**I feel even-minded and even-tempered most of the time.**

- If not, can you see a cause-and-effect relationship between possible causes and occasions of gloom, depression, worry, or even elation?

**I have come to terms with childhood memories.**

- If not, what needs to be handled?

**I have a good emotional relationship with my parents and family members.**

- If not, why not, and what could be the solution?
- If parents or other family members are not living, we can still learn to come to terms with our emotions in relationship to memories.

**I live without regret or grief.**

- If not, list the area of challenge and write a program to correct the situation.

**I forgive easily and completely.**

**I have no addictions.**

- If you do--alcohol, drugs, food, etc.-- write a program to become free from all addictions.

**I enjoy life and I enjoy relationships.**

- Again, if not, what can you do to correct matters?

**I never blame others or conditions. I always look within for guidance in order to be appropriate in all situations.**

**I rejoice in this world and I do not fear death.**

**I agree that the world seems more fair when one learns the laws of mind and consciousness.**

Use this space for any other notes relative to self-evaluation and intentional planning for useful change, if necessary. Also, write an affirmation to embody your ideal of yourself as an emotionally balanced person.

# KEYS TO EMOTIONAL WELLNESS

## Experiencing Inner Harmony

The seat, or origin, of emotions is the soul because the origin of all urges is the soul. This naturally follows because it is the soul which imparts life to mind and body. The soul enjoys, responds to survival experiences, and is inclined to withdraw from any relationship or experience which is contrary to survival. We are here speaking of a person who is not restricted by attitudes or inner conditionings.

Even during deep meditation, when mental waves are stilled and emotional surges are put to rest, we still feel peace and happiness. Emotional surges which are out of control or irrational are not useful to spiritual unfoldment and self-actualization.

When functioning without restrictions we are naturally inclined in the direction of happiness and happiness-producing experiences. When we are neurotic, or healthy-minded but with subconscious and unconscious restrictions, we behave irrationally. We sometimes may say, "I don't know why I have these strange urges and destructive reactions."

### Clearing the Mind and Emotional Life

Not only spiritual teachers, but also psychologists and other therapists who work to assist people to achieve normal function, understand the necessity of clearing the mental field and the feeling nature of distortions in order for the *perfect being* to be able to express as it is inclined to express.

Clearing can be fast or it can be slow, depending upon whether a person is willing to assume responsibility, and upon whether there is much or little material to be cleared.

It is important to understand that the real person, the being, has full responsibility to handle all patterns and conditionings in the subconscious layers of the mental field, if this responsibility will be assumed.

Too much attention given to problems only enhances our awareness of problems. Attention given to solutions results in ability to see and arrive at solutions. Major problems then become minor challenges and these can be easily solved.

The two approaches which result in clearing of mental and emotional conditionings are meditation, correctly practiced, and goals achievement. Meditation enables us to remain centered in the awareness of our real nature where no problems exist, and the achieving of worthwhile goals enables us to live in the present while planning for useful future experiences. Subconscious patterns are then altered, and former restrictive conditionings are neutralized. Memories containing traces of trauma (hurt and pain) remain as memories but without emotional content. That is, we can recall past events and experiences easily but only as useful information, without feelings of hurt, regret, loss or guilt. One of the major restricting influences for many people is the overload of pain related to memories of hurt, rejection, loss, and failure. One then attempts to avoid similar pain-causing experiences and either avoids relationships and experiences, or functions with fear of future involvements. Often, we are inclined to "forget" the past and this results in a blocking-out of large areas of mental potential. If large areas of the mental field are rendered unconscious, we then do not have the full range of the mind to use for creative projects.

Deep meditation enables us to experience the field of pure awareness; fine energy from this field then facilitates useful change and transformation in the mental field. It is far safer for one to be involved in meditation experience and goals-achievement than to be overly involved with a passive program of self-analysis. Self-analysis can be useful if it leads to understanding and mental-emotional clearing. But if we become trapped in mental and emotional patterns, we are inclined to become so introverted and problem-centered that we lose our objectivity and freedom to function.

Memories of past events or experiences are present-time memories and can be handled in present-time. Even when we vividly relive an experience through the memory process, we are still experiencing the process in the present moment.

If a memory intrudes into the conscious level of mind repeatedly, with feelings of pain and hurt, do this: Use the technique of creative imagination to vividly relive the original circumstances, but revise the conclusion so that the feeling about the circumstances is positive. You will not change the original memory; you will drain emotion from the memory. In the future, when you recall what once happened, you will do so without emotional reaction.

You can frequently *disarm* memories which contain emotional trauma merely by observing them objectively and gaining insight, without guilt and without blaming anyone.

Wherever there is pain in association with memory, we are inclined to react without thinking whenever we confront a similar situation. Clearing memories of pain is, therefore, essential. Also, learning to respond appropriately instead of reacting unconsciously is the ideal.

There are many relationships with which to come to terms if we would be emotionally well and harmoniously adjusted. For instance: are we on comfortable terms with memories of childhood? Are we on comfortable terms with parents, other memories of parents? Is there anything at all in our past that we would rather not look at or remember? Do we carry a burden of guilt about something done or not done? Do we have regrets? Do we hate others? Do we have strong likes and dislikes for no rational reason? Are we prejudiced. Are we proud? Are we forever attempting to *prove* ourselves? Are forever attempting to overtly control others and our environment? Do we have strong drives that we do not know the reasons for having? Is it important to us that others like us? Are we influenced by the opinions of others? Is the life we live the one we have chosen, or are we living someone else's dream for us? Are we comfortable about having comfort, money, love, success, and opportunity? Have we come to terms with the fact that we are really spiritual beings and that we are immortal? If we acknowledge that we are, indeed, immortal beings, what are we going to do with the rest of our life in this and other spheres, until we experience transcendental consciousness? Are we afraid of life? Are we unwilling to assume personal responsibility? Do we behave like an immature *child* or do we behave like a mature adult? Why do we do what we do? If you are now aware of certain areas in which you might be in need of clearing, write the problem, and write the possible solution. Clear that area of your memory, or your life. Use a notebook or other sheets of paper for this project.

Whenever you see the need to modify your behavior in order to be more responsible and more appropriate, decide to do so. When we regulate behavior, we can more easily take charge of thoughts and feelings because we are then totally involved in the transformation process. It may be that little matters require attention. Examples include: learning to make decisions instead of procrastinating, learning to speak more clearly and precisely in order to communicate effectively, learning to write more clearly and precisely to aid communication, following through on plans once they are agreed upon.

Never affirm that you are the victim of compulsive behavior. You are as responsible as you agree to be. To affirm, I can't help myself and I can't help what I dos to merely affirm lack of personal responsibility. Some patterns do have the driving force of the emotions behind them, but what is the source of this force? Is it not at the soul level? At the level of being?

In less enlightened eras and civilizations, people believed (some still believe) that compulsive urges and tendencies were due to the influence of demons or external agencies. Prayer and other rituals were used to banish the *demons*. When this process was effective, what really happened was that the mental and emotional conflicts were either suppressed or were cleared. This does not prove the existence of demons; it merely proves the usefulness of prayer and a more powerful flow of energy to balance the mental field and emotional. nature. Remove conflict, and health and balance are restored to the systems of the body.

Inner conflict results in disturbance from the level of mind down to the level of body function. Conflict results in physical disease by weakening the body's resistance and by altering function and chemical balance. Hypertension likewise results in interference and malfunction at various levels. Clear conflict, cure hypertension, and the body is inclined to be restored to normal function and health. Clear conflict, and the mind is inclined to function normally. Clear conflict, and one will experience emotional wellness. The most useful way to clear conflict is to become responsible, and to learn to look deeply at life and relationships and understand the process of living and the purpose for relationships. To remain undecided and allow conflict to increase is not useful. To hide from the need to make necessary changes can result in withdrawal from conscious relationships. One may, for instance, agree to live without concern about what is happening. That is, to just go along with a minimum of effort in order to experience a degree of contentment. Conversely, another way of avoiding the need to come to terms with ourselves is to become compulsively involved with projects, to be busy being busy, to be so involved with achievement that we forget the purpose of achievement. Another escape is useless social interaction. A common escape is alcoholism and drug use. Many escapists are lonely people who want fulfillment and who want to experience wholeness, but who do not know how to go about the process or who are not willing to assume responsibility, for one reason or another.

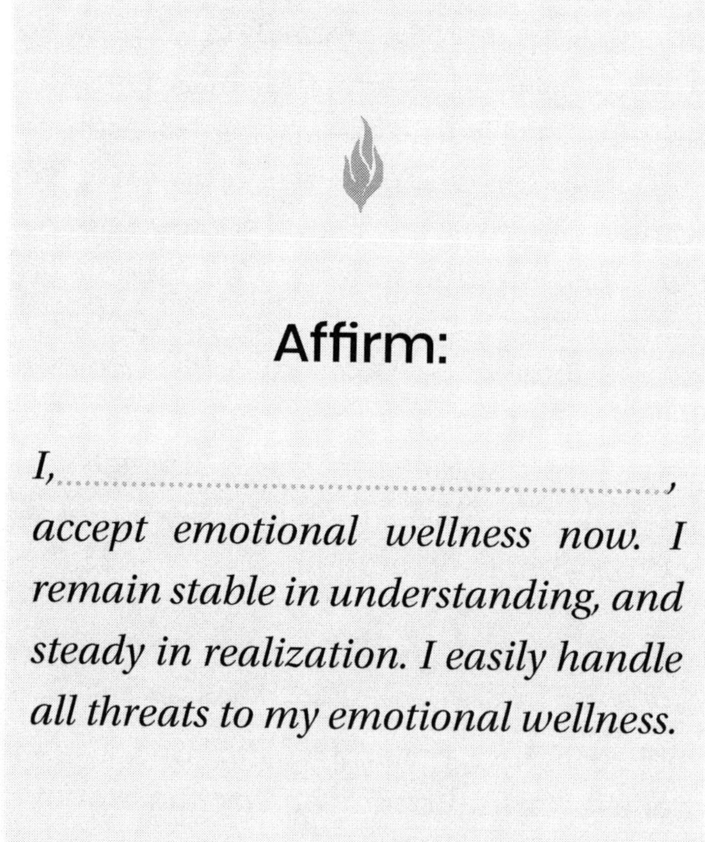

**Affirm:**

*I, ................................................................,*
*accept emotional wellness now. I remain stable in understanding, and steady in realization. I easily handle all threats to my emotional wellness.*

For a rational person to admit to incurable addiction is to make an error in judgement. Nothing has any power over us unless we consent to it. When we see a substance as merely a substance, and see it neither as good nor bad, we are then in a position to make choices regarding the use of it. When a person is dependent upon any substance or any experience in order to feel good, or high, or complete, that person is admitting that what he really seeks is the self-completeness of inner awareness and freedom from stress and conflict. There are useful things we can do to awaken awareness and to neutralize dependency upon substances, activities, and relationships which offer temporary and pseudo fulfillment. Detoxification of the body, clearing of the mind, balancing of the emotional nature, and increased soul awareness will enable any person to live freely and harmoniously in this world.

## ACTUALIZATION GUIDELINES

Practice being stable in self-understanding so that you have a positive opinion of yourself. Know that you are always a good person, regardless of what has to be cleared from the mental and emotional areas. Never allow yourself to become trapped in feelings of guilt, regret, or fear while clearing impressions relative to past experiences and relationships. Whenever you feel yourself becoming caught up in the trauma of the past, take a few deep breaths of air and center yourself. Be established in the awareness of *being*. Remind yourself that you are but clearing patterns which have nothing to do with the real you.

When clearing memories of the past, plan a time-frame in which to do it, and then complete the process and be done with it for that occasion. That is, if total clearing does not take place at one session, terminate the session and return to the process at a later time. Do not carry the process of clearing over into daily encounters or duties.

For instance, when using the creative imagination technique for revising the past, complete the cycle of action and emerge feeling complete and emotionally balanced. Or when examining past incidents, look at them and come to an understanding or an insight, and then be done with it for that occasion.

When emotional trauma is experienced and seems to persist, do this: feel the impact of the trauma and intentionally begin to breathe deeply and regularly for a few moments or a few minutes. This will tend to release energy from the memory patterns so that you experience a good feeling even while retaining the memory. By performing a body-survival action (breathing) while retaining the memory-picture, you effectively drain the trauma-energy from those memory patterns.

To avoid accumulating unwanted emotional conflicts, do this: At night, before retiring, mentally scan the events of the day from the present moment back to the first waking memory. Wherever you see where you could have improved a response or a relationship, make a decision to do so in a future situation of a similar nature. Also, as a result of this insight, release any emotional unrest relative to any mistakes or errors in judgement you might have made. Release any feelings of grief as a result of losses experienced. By using this process we are able to handle daily events on a daily basis, and remain current with full awareness. This will result in an increase of energy and more enthusiasm for living. Remember, it is often the accumulation of stress and trauma which tires the system and further conditions the mind in the direction of unconsciousness. The more conscious, the more aware we are, the greater will be our ability to handle ourselves in space and time.

Assume an attitude of mastery. A mature person can more easily handle emotional challenges than can a person who is conditioned to function as a victim. Be a master of mental and emotional states.

# GOAL ACHIEVEMENT PLAN

**Goal or Final Purpose**

**Date For Completion/Achievement:**

I complete the purpose or achieve my goal by ............................................................

**Plans For Completion and/or Achievement:**

**Obstacles Or Restrictions, If Any:**

## SOLUTIONS AND PLANS OF ACTION:

*I use these plans and experience solutions.*

**Expected Benefits as a Result of Actualizing Plans:**

# PURPOSES COMPLETED AND GOALS ACHIEVED:

**Completed/Achieved:**

Date:

**Completed/Achieved:**

Date:

**Completed/Achieved:**

Date:

*Record short-term gains and achievements as well as long-range ones.*

## GOAL OR FINAL PURPOSE

Use this page for personal notes, ideas, plans of action or for whatever useful purpose to enable you to be consciously involved with your program. You may wish to insert pictures or photos, clippings from published sources anything to assist the creative process.

# REVIEW

## Keys to Emotional Wellness

*Answer the following questions clearly:*

**What is the seat or, origin, of emotions?**

**Upon what does fast or slow clearing of the emotional condition depend?**

**What are the two approaches which result in clearing of the mental and emotional conditionings?**

**Why is it that we do not always have access to the full range of the mental field?**

**What can be done about this?**

**Describe the process of revision.**

**Why does inner conflict weaken the body's resistance?**

**Does any external thing or substance have power over us?**

**Can addictions be eradicated?**

- How can this be experienced?

# SECTION

## 5.b

## Health & Vitality

# PERSONAL EVALUATION AND PLANNING FORM

*Respond honestly to the following statements:*

**I am healthy almost all of the time.**

**I exercise on a regular schedule. List schedule and the kind of exercise performed or experienced.**

**I pay attention to a balanced, nutritional diet.**

- If not, write suggestions for improvement.

**I recognize the relationship between mental attitude, emotional wellness, and physical health and vitality.**

**I have few, if any, health-challenging habits. List them, if any. Also, write a plan for change.**

**My teeth are in excellent condition and I attend to oral health.**

**I manage stress well. If not, write a plan to manage your life so that hypertension will not be a problem for you.**

**How often do you enjoy a planned vacation?**

- What do you do when you plan your vacation and experience it?

Use this space to evaluate your health requirements and plan a program to assist you to meet your needs.

# HEALTH & VITALITY

## Regeneration & Radiant Living

The soul is superior to mental and emotional states, and mental and emotional states contribute to either health or disease. Therefore, it is essential that we be mentally clear and emotionally stable if we are to be assured of health and vitality.

If one is spiritually healthy, mental and emotional wellness will be natural and physical health will be assured. Soul force filters down from the brain, through the nervous system, into the body. Inner nourishment flows from the soul.

Stress due to conflict interferes with the flow of vital forces and restricts natural function. Study prior lessons in order to remove stress and conflict.

A willingness to be healthy and functional is essential to establishing and maintaining a health consciousness.

Exercise and rest are essential to physical health and vitality. Exercise can be tailored to individual need and capacity. Rest can involve a variety of procedures.

Exercise might be a matter of daily fast-walking, to encourage deeper breathing and force circulation of the blood throughout the system. -Other exercise routines can be running, tennis, swimming, Hatha Yoga, calisthenics, skipping rope, and so on. Also, one can include daily practice of the recharging exercises as described before.

Regular hours of restful sleep allow the body to rebuild and regenerate. Recreation which takes us away from the usual work schedule is useful as a resting-from-stress activity. Deep meditation rests not only the body but the involuntary nervous system. Learning to be aware in the moment, detached even while involved, is restful to the systems of the body.

Nutrition, suitable to personal needs and requirements, is useful in assisting the body to experience health and vitality.

There is no one *perfect* diet which will suit everyone. This is because of varying temperaments, body constitutions, daily schedules of work and activity, and genetic patterns.

A variety of natural foods, attractively prepared and taken in moderation, is the best basic rule. Balance the diet and see to providing the body with all essentials, including proteins, carbohydrates, fats, vitamins, minerals and enzymes. Avoid *fad* diets, and avoid extremes in all categories. Grains (brown rice, wheat, millet, buckwheat, corn, etc.) are basic staples. Vegetable salads and lightly cooked vegetables should be taken. Fruits in season, as well as nuts and seeds, can be taken.

If the body requires cleansing and detoxification, this can be experienced through the wise use of natural foods and other useful processes.

An easy cleansing diet is as follows: For two or three weeks follow a routine of fresh fruit for breakfast, a green salad for lunch, and another green salad for dinner, along with a serving of brown rice. The green salad should have a variety of vegetables. Dressing for the salad can be olive oil and lemon juice, with a garlic clove crushed into it. Do not use commercial salad dressing during this dietary routine. Brown rice can be seasoned with chopped onion, soy sauce, or any other natural seasoning. To prepare the brown rice, use two cups water to one cup dry rice. Bring to a boil; reduce to simmer for 20 minutes. Leave the lid on the pot during simmering. After 20 minutes, remove from heat and set aside for 20 minutes.

A more drastic cleansing fast is as follows: Prior to the fast eat only fresh fruits and raw vegetables. The evening before, take an enema. Then, for one week take freshly squeezed fruit juice for early morning hours. Afternoon, take freshly squeezed vegetable juice. The fruit juices can be apple, pineapple, pear, or any other juice desired, except citrus. Vegetable juices can be carrot juice as a base, with any green vegetables juiced and added. For a hot broth, at noon or in the evening, do the following: Cut potatoes, carrots, celery, onions, etc. into small cubes and simmer for 30 minutes. Remove from heat and allow to set for 30 minutes. Strain the broth. Drink while warm. Store extra in the refrigerator for later use. Herb tea can be taken, also, with honey. When coming off the fast, add a bit of fruit the first day, while remaining on the juice routine. The second day, add a steamed or lightly cooked vegetable for lunch and dinner. Gradually return to a normal diet. Take an enema every day or two during the fast. Also, walk briskly and breathe deeply while walking. Bathe at least twice a day and scrub the skin with a towel to remove dead cells and keep the pores open so that perspiration may flow easily.

During cleansing diet routines and fasting, meditate more and become inwardly aware that your body is more and more reliant upon the vital force of the soul. Avoid vitamins and other food supplements while fasting. Do not fast if you are already under the care of a physician who is supervising a diet plan for your special needs, such as a blood sugar problem.

## Healing of the Body

Remember that the intelligence within you is inclined to work to insure health of all systems and organs of the body. If there is need for healing of the body, if there is need for encouraging the body systems to function more effectively, use the following method:

Meditate for the purpose of relaxation until you experience peace and serenity.

Visualize (picture) your body as healthy and fully functional in all respects. If there is a specific condition that needs healing, visualize that condition as clearing and inwardly *see* and feel perfect health and perfect function.

Rest for a while in this feeling of wholeness. Feel good about it. Rejoice. Be happy.

Emerge from the practice session and maintain this attitude and inner knowing that all is well.

In serious conditions it would be well to work with a qualified member of one of the healing arts in order to have support and encouragement, and to have improvement monitored.

Even if healing is not needed, one can use the above method to improve the *mental picture* of the body. While relaxed, visualize yourself at the ideal body weight, full of energy, and vital in all ways. As you do this you will unfold a consciousness of health which will release vital forces into the system, as well as prompt you to abide by the laws of health which can contribute to wellness and health.

Remember to support yourself in your plans for healthy and vital living by maintaining a positive attitude about yourself and about life. Avoid thoughts, feelings, and activities which are destructive as you train yourself to cultivate thoughts, feelings, and behavior which contribute to function. Bear in mind that mental attitude and emotional health both strongly contribute to physical health and vitality. Even if you already know the guidelines as suggested here, be sure to put useful suggestions into practice as they relate to your personal life and needs.

## Affirm:

*I, ..............................................................................................,*
*do now enter into an agreement with myself to do all that is essential in order to experience true health and vitality.*

# ACTUALIZATION GUIDELINES

## Goal Achievement Plan

Here is an exercise to use to encourage a greater flow of energy through the body. After meditation, before stopping the process, let your feelings come down into the body and feel the body inside and outside. Learn to become aware of the inner spaces of the body. Feel and visualize that vital force is flowing down from the brain to fill the body through and through; this is soul force which nourishes and regulates all body processes.

Feel that fine superconscious forces are saturating every system, every organ, and every cell of your body. Every atom is filled with light. Inwardly visualize your body as light. The light of the soul, the light of you, and the body as light is one whole.

Feel that the mental field is cleared, the nervous system is refined, and the body is purified by this downflowing light and power. Nerve force flows down to infiltrate the body. Prana flows down to nourish the subtle aspects of your body and is distributed through the chakras which correspond, at a finer level, to the major nerve centers in the spinal pathway.

As you practice this process more and more, you will always be aware that you are a being of light even while you function through the physical body.

Bear in mind that while you will not live forever in your present physical body, you can live this present life in health. Do not allow beliefs or acquired habits to interfere with this fact. As a soul you are superior to mind and body. The body must reflect your inner realization of wholeness. Do not be limited by any claim to the contrary. Do all that you can to live in harmony with natural laws and to encourage the natural process of function and health.

**Goal or Final Purpose:**

**Date For Completion/Achievement:**

I complete the purpose or achieve my goal by ______.

**Plans For Completion and/or Achievement:**

**Obstacles Or Restrictions, If Any:**

## SOLUTIONS AND PLANS OF ACTION:

*I use these plans and experience solutions.*

**Expected Benefits as A Result of Actualizing Plans:**

**Purposes Completed and Goals Achieved:**

**Completed/Achieved:**

Date:

**Completed/Achieved:**

Date:

**Completed/Achieved:**

Date:

*Record short-term gains and achievements as well as long-range ones.*

Use this page for personal notes, ideas, plans of action, or other useful purpose to enable yourself to be consciously involved with your program. You may wish to insert pictures or photos, clippings from published sources, or anything else that would assist your creative process.

# REVIEW

## Health & Vitality

*Respond clearly to the following questions and directives:*

**Why is it essential that we be mentally clear and emotionally stable if we are to experience health and vitality?**

**Where does inner nourishment come from?**

**Outline an easy cleansing-diet routine.**

## When should one not fast?

**Review the process for releasing healing forces in the system.**

# SECTION

## 6.[a]

## Relationships

# PERSONAL EVALUATION AND PLANNING FORM

*Write your response to these statements and directives.*

**Describe the word *love* in your own words.**

**I feel comfortable in a stable relationship.**

- If not, write the area of challenge and possible solutions.

**I feel a sense of kinship with all life.**

**I am willing to nourish and support others and I am willing to receive nourishment and support from them.**

**I believe that all things work together for good when correctly understood.**

**I am willing to modify my behavior when I find that it is the correct and useful thing to do.**

**I see the One Life expressing through all people.**

**Regardless of the behavior or the attitude of others I always do the correct and appropriate thing.**

**I have come to terms with the past, I live joyously in the present, and I look forward to the glorious future.**

**I appreciate nature and the workings of nature.**

**My reverence for life fully embraces all living creatures.**

**I look for the good in others, always, and call it forth.**

**Write an affirmation which can be useful to you in experiencing fully supportive relationships with people and your world:**

# RELATIONSHIPS

## Open And Supportive Sharing

### Relationships are Essential

As long as we function in a relative world relationship we cannot help but relate. Even if we were to withdraw from the company of other human beings, a relationship with nature would still exist. And, as long as one is still seeking Self-realization, a relationship between soul and God will have to be explored and experienced.

The world in which we live is made possible because of relationships. Everything in nature is mutually inter dependent. Planet Earth is one organic whole, an entity.

When we eat food we take in energy and convert it to our body's use. We are emotionally nourished by other people who care for us and we nourish those for whom we care and with whom we have a relationship.

Until full realization is experienced man will consciously or unconsciously be on a quest for God-realization. This quest cannot be forever avoided.

Where there is full communication there is also a total working relationship. Communication can be learned and cooperative working relationships can be experienced.

Some people find it difficult to communicate because of emotional immaturity, fear of rejection, or conditioned patterns which block the flow of communication. Experience and willingness to learn to communicate will enable one to outgrow emotional immaturity. As we learn to communicate effectively in a mature and supportive-manner, fear of rejection will cease to influence our behavior. Subconscious and deep unconscious conditionings which prevent open and supportive communication can be cleared from the mental field and the emotional life.

For communication between people to be total there must be an agreement to communicate, there must be understanding, and there must be a flow between those communicating. If any of these three essentials are lacking, communication is not complete.

Even without a strong emotional bond, if mature people will agree to communicate for a mutual purpose, there can be a supportive and understanding relationship for the common good.

We all have something in common: our unique nature as consciousness. We are all units of the same Oversoul. Therefore, we are designed to interact and to be mutually supportive. Even if we must communicate and relate with persons whose attitudes and opinions differ from our own, we can still relate with non-judgmental respect. By seeing the truth about ourselves and others we are able to allow others the freedom to be themselves as they work out their own destiny. We should maintain our own freedom, also. A supportive relationship does not result in anyone being used, hurt, or exploited.

When we understand that all persons are expressions of the one Life we will not ever think in terms of using or of injuring another person. Nor, will we allow ourselves to play the role of being a victim.

Not every relationship is meant to be a permanent one. But, for as long as such a relationship continues it can be open and supportive.

To pray for the welfare of others is useful, for them and for ourselves. Prayer in this fashion purifies the heart, the feeling nature, and removes tendencies and patterns which interfere with supportive communication.

## Clearing Relationships

To enjoy open (clear) relationships there must be effective communication. If any necessary relationship is not open, then clear it by doing your part to ensure effective communication. Come to an agreement and understanding relative to what is expected in a relationship for the mutual good. If this is impossible, you may need to terminate the relationship.

When we think in terms of the mutual good we can usually come to terms in a relationship and agree upon what is to be expected by every person involved. Think in terms of benefit (support) for every person involved.

If you have done all that you can honestly do to ensure an open and supportive working relationship, and the other person has not or will not, and if it is obvious that there is no point in pursuing the attempt to communicate, the relationship can be terminated without regret and without hurt feelings.

To fail to terminate a non-useful relationship is often to play the role of being a victim.

Once a supportive relationship has been established, do all you can do to maintain it and keep your agreements with all who are involved. In other words, be honest in the relationship. Be true to yourself and be true to others.

As long as we work from the level of conditioned mind, as long as we function as a personality, we are inclined to attempt to fulfill our ego-needs in a relationship. First, come to terms with yourself as a spiritual being and then live and relate from that understanding.

For many people, a relationship means *I will overlook your faults as long as you overlook mine.* And, *I will try to meet your psychological needs if you try to meet mine and attempt to make me a whole person by filling in the missing spaces in my psyche.* This type of relationship can be observed at all levels of society, but it is not a mature relationship, and does not lead to self-actualization and spiritual fulfillment.

To relate out of need almost always results in compromise. To relate in order to experience unfoldment and the fulfillment of potential leads to mature relationships. Learn to establish priorities in relationships. Enter into relationships which can result in mutual growth and benefit.

Self-respect and respect for others is a sound basis for a relationship. Husbands and wives who respect each other will communicate and relate appropriately. Family members who respect each other will ensure domestic harmony and encourage personal growth. Where there is mutual respect, in the community, in a work environment, between people in all walks of life who relate for a common purpose, there will be agreement, support and nourishment for the soul.

## Practical Things to Do

Make a list of all of the things you can do to more fully support and nourish people with whom you relate. Immediately put into practice the suggestions you have written for yourself. Look for the good in others and call it forth through appropriate behavior, ideal speech, and supportive response. When others need an assist, when they need a boost, if at all possible lend an assist and help them to become the whole beings they really desire to be.

Let your caring extend to all living creatures. Awaken to a realization of a reverence for life in all forms. Nourish your personal environment and contribute to the health of the planet in all ways.

Your relationship with world consciousness is also a personal responsibility. So live your life, with the ideal mental attitude and state of consciousness, that you silently radiate uplift and strength to planetary consciousness. In this way you contribute to the unfoldment of all mankind. Learn to see the hand of God at work in every expression of life and in every relationship.

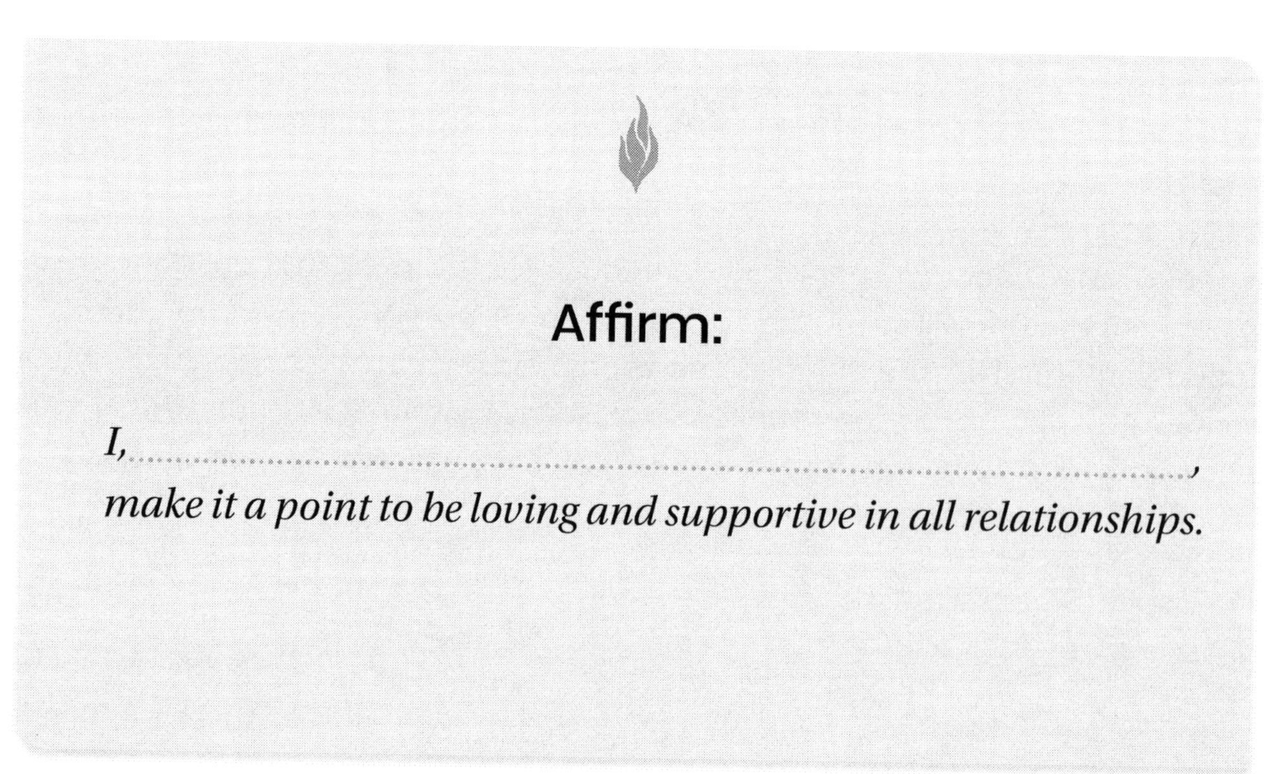

# ACTUALIZATION GUIDELINES

After meditation, visualize and feel that you are on harmonious terms with all of the forces in nature and with every creature and every person on the planet. Make this your realization.

If you have not cleared any relationship, past or present, do what you can do to accomplish this as soon as possible.

Do something supportive for those near to you. Let them know you love them by your actions. Expect nothing in return, but be able to accept any supportive action which is given you. When we expect but do not receive, we can allow ourselves to be hurt. Give and be open to your good but do not demand anything of another. Life will provide you with nourishment and support if you are open to it.

See a human need and fill it: when you see a hurt, do your part to heal it.

If you are on good terms with yourself, you will find it easy to be on good terms with others. Work on yourself, if necessary.

Never try to change others. Set an ideal example to others and call forth the inner nature of those with whom you relate.

Good comes *through* other people, it never comes *from* them. Good flows to others through you; it never originates with you.

## When working with others, think like this:

- *Am I honest?*
- *Am I fair?*
- *Am I selfless?*
- *Am I supportive?*

When in conflict with another, and when tempted to communicate in anger or to hurt, be alone until you become calm and then communicate with reason and fairness. Never take advantage of another person and never try to get even. Forgive, release, and relate in the ideal manner, always.

Speak, write, and communicate in all ways clearly and completely. Lack of complete communication is a major barrier to open and supportive relationships. Be attentive to clear communication.

If you pray for others, you cannot have enemies. If you are having difficulty with a person, do not pray for him to change to suit your needs; pray for his highest good.

" "

***Open and supportive relationships begin with us.***

***We are responsible for our relationships.***

# GOAL ACHIEVEMENT PLAN

**Goal or Final Purpose:**

**Date For Completion/Achievement:**

I complete the purpose or achieve my goal by ________.

**Plans For Completion and/or Achievement:**

## Obstacles Or Restrictions, If Any:

## SOLUTIONS AND PLANS OF ACTION:

*I use these plans and experience solutions.*

**Expected Benefits as a Result of Actualizing Plans:**

**Purposes Completed and Goals Achieved:**

**Completed/Achieved:**

Date:

**Completed/Achieved:**

Date:

**Completed/Achieved:**

Date:

*Record short-term gains and achievements as well as long-range ones.*

# GOAL OR FINAL PURPOSE

Use this page for personal notes, ideas, plans of action, or other useful purpose to enable yourself to be consciously involved with your program. You may wish to insert pictures or photos, clippings from published sources, or anything else that would assist your creative process.

# REVIEW

## Relationships

*Answer the following questions clearly.*

**Why is it important to learn to experience open and supportive relationships?**

**What is essential to a total working relationship?**

## What can one do to outgrow emotional immaturity?

**Can people have a supportive and understanding relationship if no strong emotional bond exists?**

- If so, why?

## What do we all have in common?

**Why is prayer useful for us?**

**Is it ever correct to terminate a relationship?**

- If so, when?

**What is a sound basis for a relationship?**

**What can we do to contribute to the unfoldment of all mankind?**

# SECTION

## 6.b

## YOUR RIGHT PLACE IN LIFE

# PERSONAL EVALUATION AND PLANNING FORM

*Write your response to each statement.*

**I feel content that I am in my right place in life.**

**I feel that I am fulfilling my destiny.**

**There are things I have not done yet, and I plan to do them in this present life-cycle.**

- List them.

**I accept the doctrine of reincarnation.**

- If so, explain the doctrine as you understand it.
- If not, explain why not, or why it makes no difference to you.

**I believe I will continue to live as a conscious being after I depart from this earth.**

- If so, explain.
- If not, explain.

**I believe that some people are drawn together in order to experience the fulfillment of mutual agreements and destinies.**

- If so, explain.

**I accept the idea that there is a Larger Plan that helps to determine the personal destiny of people and mankind as a whole.**

**If so, explain.**

- If not, explain why not.

**I can see evidence that world consciousness is awakening. I see how I can participate in this process in the direction of world transformation by:**

# YOUR RIGHT PLACE IN LIFE

## Fulfillment Of Personal Destiny

### Our Appointment with Destiny

There are two purposes for our having come into the world. One, we are here to learn lessons and to awaken to the realization of the truth about life. Two, we are here to render useful service to others and assist the evolutionary process.

The lessons we have come to learn while in this world have to do with working in harmony with the laws of mind and consciousness. By acquiring accurate information and then testing ourselves in the world we learn to actualize what we learn. We experience fulfillment and we become able to assist others in a realistic manner.

Success in utilizing the principles of mind and consciousness in order to function in the world is a major lesson; equally important is that we examine the nature of consciousness and awaken to full realization of the reality of God and our relationship with God.

Since we share this world with others, one of our purposes while here is to assist other people in their enlightenment quest. Also, we are to assist others to experience the fulfillment of their personal needs so that they may have peace of mind and a firm foundation upon which to unfold their inner soul potential.

Fate has to do with cause and effect. We are fated, sooner or later, to experience the effects of prior causes unless we modify or eradicate the influence of such causes. A cause-and-effect pattern can continue for many years in time and space and can so bind a person that the fulfillment of destiny is delayed. Destiny has to do with why we are really here. When we awaken to an awareness of why we are here we can then begin to work in the direction of the fulfillment of destined purposes even while working within the framework of cause and effect. patterns. It would be folly to affirm that we will first learn to be free from cause-and-effect patterns before embarking upon the path of destined fulfillment. To begin a conscious move in the direction of the fulfillment of destiny conveniently orders our life and modifies unwanted and destructive cause and effect influences.

Growth is natural to life. The more aware we become the more we expand our awareness to include greater areas of life. I am not saying *that bigger is better*, only that it is natural for us to become more cosmic as we unfold our potential. If we do not grow, if we do not expand our awareness, we either become less conscious or we are inclined to remain overly involved with routine and non-result-producing matters. We assure growth and unfoldment as we apply the principles we learn in a meaningful fashion.

How do we find our right place in life? How do we know when we are fulfilling the purposes for which we have come? If we do not feel fulfilled, what can we do to assist the awakening process so that we can find our right place in life?

We know that we are in our right place in life when we feel a deep inner satisfaction which results from a life well lived. It is important that we be possessed of a firm inner awareness of our nature as a spiritual being. If we do not have this as a basis, we will be inclined to be discontent regardless of how well and how harmonious our relationships and activities are. When everything is flowing well and we still feel lack of contentment, what is needed is to deepen the spiritual life through prayer and meditation.

Everything flows from within. Therefore, no matter how outwardly successful we are, if we are not grounded in soul-awareness we will not be fulfilled. Even outer success may then seem empty. A useful process is to affirm, after meditation and whenever needed during the day, *I am now in my right place in life*. Affirm with feeling until inner contentment is experienced. This will result in ideas and activities which conform to the inner realization. This may seem a simplistic process but it works. Try it, experience it, and see the results for yourself. Invite others to use the process also.

There are people in all walks of life, in every age group, who are not inwardly comfortable with themselves because they have not yet found their place in life. At a deep level, you already know what you have come to do. You may have allowed superficial involvements to lead you into a life pattern which has taken you away from the path of life you were destined to follow. It is never too late to change; it is never too late to make useful choices. Would that we all were able to awaken to the awareness of our mission in life at an early age! However, we are dealing with the moment. We are handling matters from this present opportunity of decision.

A word here about young people. If you have the opportunity of working with young adults, why not encourage them to search within for the answers relative to their life's work? Why not really educate them by showing them how to release from deeper levels the true guidance which can teach them every step of the way how to make life worthwhile, and how to make a major contribution to the world?

## Is It Necessary to Believe in Prior Existence?

It is obvious, when we sincerely examine the matter, that we did not have our beginning at conception or at birth of the physical body. If we had a beginning, we would have an end. No deeply-aware person feels this to be true. No enlightened teacher has said this was true. Even if we do not have true understanding about how the soul moves through time and space on its journey to completion, we inwardly know that we are immortal beings, because our basic nature is consciousness and consciousness has no beginning or end. There was a *beginning* relative to when we first identified with nature but, before that, we existed in the realm of pure consciousness. We will, according to enlightenment teachings, continue to function in the relative spheres until we fulfill our destiny and awaken to the realm of pure consciousness once more. It is not necessary to *believe* in prior existence because, at the soul level, we already *know* we are immortal.

There is, likewise, no point in debating the doctrine of reincarnation. Again, enlightenment teachers teach it but they do not emphasize it because the important matter at hand is living our present life well and doing our duty with surrendered understanding. There are many people who feel they have come with a specific work to do. They are born with a sense of destiny and, as soon as they are able, they begin their work. They often attract others who have a common purpose. Thus, it is felt that some souls meet time and time again to cooperate in useful projects for world good. If this happens, it happens. I feel it is useful to remain attuned with God's will and follow inner guidance, then allow outer relationships and patterns to unfold. Who does anything? It is the one Life which does everything through extensions of Itself.

An awareness of life as extending beyond this life-cycle can greatly contribute to one's sense of purpose. After we complete our duties here, what then? This present phase on earth is but a preparation for something else. We are wise, then, to do all we can do to pre pare ourselves for the future by consciously attending to essential matters while the opportunity is before us. We work for the good of our world because we feel the world is worth supporting. It is worth supporting so that we are more secure, and so that those who follow us will have a greater opportunity to express themselves and to know freedom and happiness. If we did not feel that man deserved an assist, we would live selfishly; but it is not man's nature to be selfish. I refer here to a person who is not suffering from internal conflicts.

No fulfillment of destiny can be experienced without self-honesty and integrity. If we are not honest with ourselves, we will be inclined to remain involved in superficial role-playing relationships. If we lack integrity, we will not have the moral strength to live in a responsible manner with other people or world conditions. Spiritual and emotional maturity are necessary if we are to remain anchored in life as we handle all matters which require our responsible involvement Scriptures worldwide share guidelines for living an honest and moral life. Without honesty and morality, even if we were to attain increased mental powers we would not be sure of making a useful contribution to our world. We might, instead, merely extend our immature influence and do more harm than good, as well as complicate our own lives and the lives of others. Honesty and integrity must extend into every area of living and must be the foundation upon which all relationships rest. When we are self-honest, we do not attempt to pretend that needs are not present and that change is not required. It is only through honest evaluation and deep inner transformation that we can hope to experience cleansing so that soul nature can express.

## Practical Things to Do

Philosophical discussion is useful, but the great essential, the matter of prime importance, is coming to terms with all that relates to our destiny.

Read, study and contemplate, of course. But, to come to terms with destiny get involved with the process of living.

Think in long-range terms. Take care of present duties and plan wisely for the near and distant future. Then, think in terms of the world condition long after your presence here. Will the world be a better place because you passed this way? I am not suggesting that you leave behind any kind of visible monument to yourself, unless it will have some inspirational value to others. But, will you have done your all to raise the consciousness of the world and to insure the health of the planet?

To be very practical, have you made your will or arranged for the prudent handling of your estate? If you are a person of influence in an organization, have you made plans for a smooth and competent person or team to carry on without you?

Have you realized the difference between your wants and your needs? Have you determined the difference between what is important in your life and what is not important?

Has each relationship that you have experienced been as honest and as useful as it should have been? I mean, do you handle a relationship (or a project) completely, without any loose ends and without having to go back to correct anything?

Have you removed from your life everything that might prevent you from achieving your goals and realizing your purposes?

Does your concern for assisting others and your world begin at home, with those who are with you and with whom you share your life? It starts here. If the domestic scene is not yet cleared so that harmony is the rule, don't let this stop you from moving on to useful projects, but do attend to duty at home and heal whatever needs to be healed.

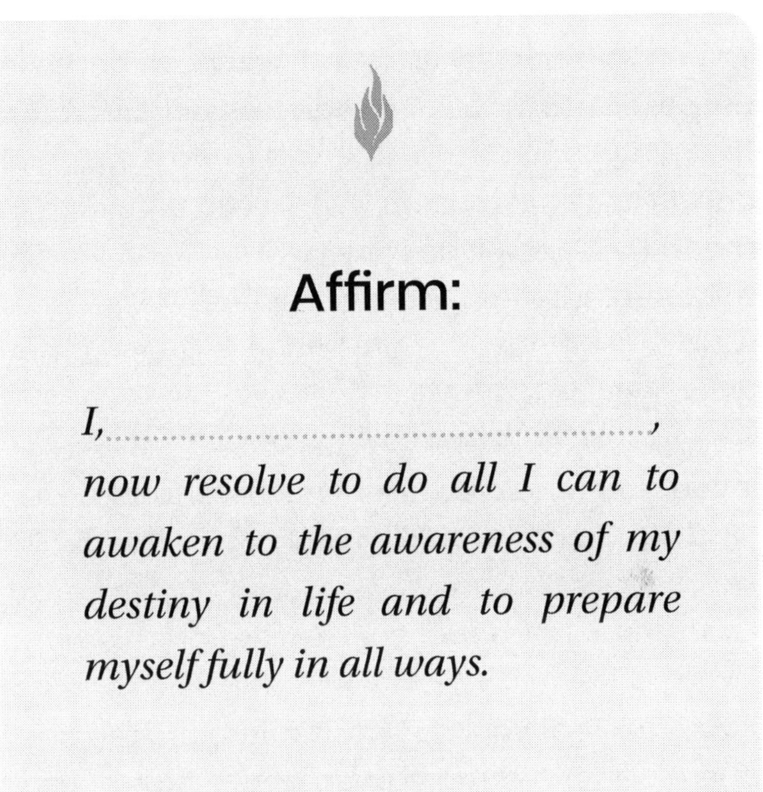

**Affirm:**

*I, ..............................................,*
*now resolve to do all I can to awaken to the awareness of my destiny in life and to prepare myself fully in all ways.*

Prepare yourself now for fulfilling your destiny. Plan now and do all you can to meet opportunity when it presents itself. See to your education; learn the principles; make needed inner and outer changes; acquire experience. The more capable you are, the more effective you will be when you begin to move consciously in harmony with the patterns which will assist you in the direction of total completion.

## ACTUALIZATION GUIDELINES

You have a destiny with God. You have come into this world for a useful purpose. Find that purpose, and function as you were meant to function. It may be that your destiny is to play the role you already know and to do it well, with all of the talent and ability you have. This can, in itself, be a useful exercise in unfolding innate potential. Greatness does not always mean that we will be known for the extra ordinary things we do; it may mean that we are to do ordinary things extraordinarily well. Enlightenment can be experienced by one in any walk of life. Heaven is present in fullness at any given moment and in any given situation when we see clearly.

If you do not yet feel that you have found your destined place in life, assist someone else who has; contribute to their energies and projects.

Order your life so that you can depart this world without regret.

If you feel that your destiny is related to the destiny pattern of others, list those other people and enter into a more open and useful working relationship with them. Write their names here and make notes relative to how you can improve your relationship.

If you feel led to do a thing but lack education and practical skills, acquire that education and develop those skills. Pay someone to teach you, if that is necessary. Obtain books and useful data and tools. Invest in yourself for your future good. You have already invested in yourself by participating in this program. Are you making the most of your opportunity?

Be sure to inwardly feel, always, *I am now in my right place in life. God is my companion in all that I am led to do.* When you are established in this realization, because the inner reflects as the outer, you will find yourself lead into the right paths in life, and all that is required for the fulfillment of destiny will come to you. This may seem a simplistic idea, but it is true.

# GOAL ACHIEVEMENT PLAN

**Goal or Final Purpose:**

**Date For Completion/Achievement:**

I complete the purpose or achieve my goal by .

**Plans For Completion and/or Achievement:**

## Obstacles Or Restrictions, If Any:

## SOLUTIONS AND PLANS OF ACTION:

*I use these plans and experience solutions.*

**Expected Benefits As A Result Of Actualizing Plans:**

**Purposes Completed and Goals Achieved:**

**Completed/Achieved:**

Date:

**Completed/Achieved:**

Date:

**Completed/Achieved:**

Date:

*Record short-term gains and achievements as well as long-range ones.*

Use this page for personal notes, ideas, plans of action or for whatever useful purpose to enable you to be consciously involved with your program. You may wish to insert pictures or photos, clippings from published sources ,anything to assist the creative process.

# REVIEW

## Your Right Place in Life

**What are the two purposes for our being in this world?**

**What is the difference between fate and destiny?**

**How do we know when we are in our right place in life?**

**What can we do to find our right place in life?**

**How can we assist young people who are looking for direction?**

**Did we ever have a beginning?**

- If so, when?

**Why are we naturally inclined to be selfless in relationships?**

**Can the fulfillment of destiny be experienced without honesty and integrity?**

- What does it mean to have integrity?

**What can you do now to prepare for the unfoldment of your innate potential and to experience the fulfillment of destiny?**

# SECTION

## 7.ª

## PROSPERITY

# Definitions

**Self-realization**: living from the conscious awareness of being the true Self

**true Self**: one's true identity as an individualized unit of the one Reality (God); other than a mistaken sense of self-identity

# PERSONAL EVALUATION AND PLANNING FORM

## PROSPERITY

*Respond honestly to the following statements:*

**I feel worthy of being prosperous.**

**I feel it is natural and easy to move through this world.**

**I render service, and I am compensated accordingly, fairly, and in abundance.**

**I enjoy finding needs and filling them.**

**I experience life as a wonderful adventure.**

**I tithe a portion of my resources for the upliftment and education of others.**

**I am attentive to a planned program of savings and investments.**

**I am a prudent steward of the goods which have been provided me.**

**I pay my bills promptly and with gratitude.**

**I use my time and energy wisely, always.**

**I know that the substance (energy) of this world is inexhaustible.**

**I rejoice in the success and prosperity of others.**

**I am always open to my unplanned good fortune, knowing that life has many ways to meet my needs and is willing to do so when I am open and receptive.**

**Life has been good to me, and I am good to life.**

**I realize fully that freedom of expression is natural to me when I am open and responsive to life.**

**Write an affirmation which would be useful to assist you in maintaining a prosperity attitude and consciousness. A sample here follows:**

“ ”

*There is Reality, one Being, one Life, one Substance, one Power in, as, and through the world. Life can and life does meet my every need, on time and in abundance. I am thankful for this experience.*

# TRUE AND LASTING PROSPERITY

## Guidelines to Personal Freedom

### What Does It Mean to Prosper?

To *prosper* means to thrive, to flourish. to be successful. Are you thriving? Are you flourishing? Are you successful? If so, you are prospering. If not, you are not prospering. Life is inclined in the direction of unfoldment, of thriving, of flourishing, of moving in the direction of fulfillment of purposes. Life is inclined in the direction of success.

Any conscious and rational person can, if he wants to do so, prosper in all ways. If you are willing to do what must be done to prosper, you can prosper.

True prosperity is reflected in our lives as spiritual awareness, mental creativity, emotional wellness, physical health and vitality, open and supportive human relationships, and freedom to express in this world.

If we are restricted or limited in any way, we are not prospering. Therefore, restrictions must be eliminated and limitations banished from our lives.

When we prosper, we not only fulfill our personal destiny; we are then able to more fully assist others and our awakening world in worthwhile way.

One great saint said, "Few mortals know that the kingdom of heaven extends fully to this earth plane." Heaven is a word which means fulfillment, order and harmony. Fulfillment, order, and harmony can be our experience in this and all worlds, spheres, planes and dimensions once we are firmly settled in true understanding. The great master, Paramahansa Yogananda, said, "Prosperity does not always mean that we get what we want. It means to have what we need, when we need it."

To be mortal is to be anchored in material consciousness and subject to mental conditionings, beliefs, concepts, and opinions. Anyone so restricted cannot even imagine how it would be to experience total freedom.

We can, with discernment, learn to tell the difference between ego-wants and true useful desires and needs for ideal living. It is a common experience among enlightened men and women that even small wants are gratified. When we say *having what we need when we need it*, we are not affirming living at the level of bare survival; rather we are emphasizing the fact that life is responsive and will meet us at our level of current need and acceptance.

You are destined, sooner or later, to experience prosperity.

Before we can prosper, we must remove restricting patterns and conditions, from within ourselves and also from our environment. Unless this is accomplished, we will be forever working against limiting conditions.

## Common restrictions include:

- Fear of success.
- Fear of possible failure if a project is attempted.
- The *will* to die or to become unconscious.
- Fear of what others might say when our life changes -.
- The belief that it is wrong to prosper.
- The feeling that to prosper is contrary to spiritual values.
- Unwillingness to enter into an intentional program leading to a true and lasting prosperous life.
- Laziness, lack of purpose, and lack of discipline.
- The company of negative and failure-directed people.

The list of common restrictions is almost endless, and includes every inner and outer situation that is contrary to life's natural inclination in the direction of unfoldment.

Many people fear success because they are afraid of the personal responsibility that might go with it. Do not fear failure. Be rightly resolved. Even if you make a mistake you can learn lessons from that experience and you will learn to avoid future mistakes. Some people have such a resistance to life that they are strongly death-directed; their will to live is minimal. Learning to see life as a great adventure can neutralize this condition. Our life is ours to live, and we cannot waste our time pleasing others who, themselves, are restricted and who do not understand our inner needs and drives. The belief that it is wrong to prosper is the result of faulty thinking. The feeling that to prosper is contrary to spiritual values is also the result of faulty thinking. To be consumed with a drive to master the material universe is error, of course. To understand that our duty is to wisely handle ourselves in space and time is wisdom. Unwillingness to enter into a useful intentional program which could lead to freedom is to be a slave to inertia and personal habits. Laziness, lack of purpose, and lack of needed discipline are characteristics of an immature personality. To associate with people who are negative and who are not inclined in the direction of fulfillment, success and prosperity is destructive. Either educate them to a higher way of life or no longer associate with them. They have their destiny; you have yours.

When we remove restricting patterns from our mental and emotional lives, we find that we are naturally inclined to function in the most ideal and appropriate manner in all relationships. One might follow the advice of successful people to the letter, relative to outer rules; but if a prosperity attitude and a prosperity consciousness is not acquired there is no possibility of experiencing true and lasting prosperity. Millions of inspirational books have been distributed throughout the world for decades but only a few, among the many readers, have made that adjustment from a consciousness of limitation to a lasting consciousness of wholeness which, alone, can result in fulfillment.

# CULTIVATING A PROSPERITY ATTITUDE AND CONSCIOUSNESS

In the successful cultivation of a prosperity consciousness the great essential is *mental attitude*. How one looks at life and how one really thinks about life determines mental attitude. What is your mental attitude about yourself in relationship to your world? Do you want to be successful? Do you want to thrive, to flourish, to experience unfoldment after unfoldment? Or, are you content to accept what fate provides? Remember, our emphasis is upon total health and total function, on all levels. When we refer to prosperity we are not just referring to economic health, as important as this is.

*Self-esteem*, a healthy self-image, is basic to ultimate fulfillment. Even more permanent than self-image is Self-realization, living from the conscious awareness of being the true Self.

Whenever you discern any inner resistance to the ideal of fulfillment, immediately clear it from mind and feelings. Practice making needed adjustments in attitude, thinking and feeling. Allow constructive action to result in success and achievement, and this will change unwanted patterns.

Use affirmations, when necessary, to awaken inner awareness and realization. When discouraged, practice meditation and creative imagination until you are again stabilized in a constructive and useful mental attitude.

## Actualizing The Laws Of Success

If we will abide by the laws of success, we are certain to be successful. The principles have to be used intelligently in order for us to acquire experience. Here are some suggestions:

- Use the goal planning forms provided with this program.

- Pay attention to the principles of success which relate to every area of your life.
- Control your verbal conversations. Never again say such things as, *Money isn't everything.* Or, *Not all people were meant to prosper and perhaps I'm one of them.* Of course, money isn't everything. No thing is everything. But we should be able to easily handle any form of substance or energy if we are to be free in this world. See through all forms and symbols to that which is Real, then wisely handle the stuff of this world.
- Learn to think in terms of rendering real service to others and your world. As you find your area of service you will experience fulfillment and automatic success. Study again the lesson on "Fulfillment of Personal Destiny" to learn how to find your right place in life and to become aware of your special service to others.
- In all that you do, work with the Power that directs all of the energies in the universe. In all that you do, remember that life's inclination is to move in the direction of fulfillment. When you are attuned to life's inclination you are certain to prosper and be fulfilled.
- Economic freedom is essential. If your needs are minimal in order for you to fulfill your purpose, as long as you have whatever is required to function and be successful, you are prosperous. If your needs are greater in order for you to fulfill you purpose, if you are open to life's goodness and if you do your part, you will experience an abundance of all that is required to function and be successful. Life knows nothing of smallness and largeness. Life is already all in all. Life contains everything and is everything. Concepts of limitation are ours, only. If you really feel led to do a thing, and find that you are restricted in any way, you are in need of inner changes in attitude and consciousness. Life would not inspire you to do a useful thing if life were not already willing to provide all of the essentials for that thing to be done. Any limitation, therefore, is within us if we are unable to move forward in the direction of completion. This is no *fault* of ours, it merely shows that change is indicated.
- Realize that all you need for prosperous living is already available and can be appropriated and utilized.
- If you earn money in exchange for hours expended, then how you spend your money is how you spend your hours (your life and energy). As you render true service you are entitled to fair compensation in some form.
- In most societies money is the accepted medium of exchange. Learn to handle money wisely, without fear and without grasping at it. Learn to direct the flow of money so that you accomplish the most useful results.
- Think in terms of abundance and surplus rather that in terms of limitation and lack.
- Retain a portion of all you earn and invest it wisely.

- Give, without thought of reward, a portion of what you earn or have to an enlightenment cause for the betterment of your world. You are a spiritual conduit on earth for the wise distribution of substance and wealth.
- Accept the truth that you can move freely through time and space in this world. If you want to be somewhere, mentally see yourself as being there at the appropriate time, and then plan to be there. This law works whether you are planning a trip to a distant city, or country, or across town. Desires fulfill themselves and real needs are met, on time and harmoniously. Train yourself to think like this.

There is one power, one being, one substance in, as, and through this world: God. Always work in relationship to this truth. If you do, you will experience fulfillment on all levels and know true and lasting prosperity.

- The Power directs the universal process.
- The Being is the Reality, the Life.
- The Substance is the energy flowing from consciousness.
- These three aspects of the Oversoul are involved in the universal process and there are no other influences.

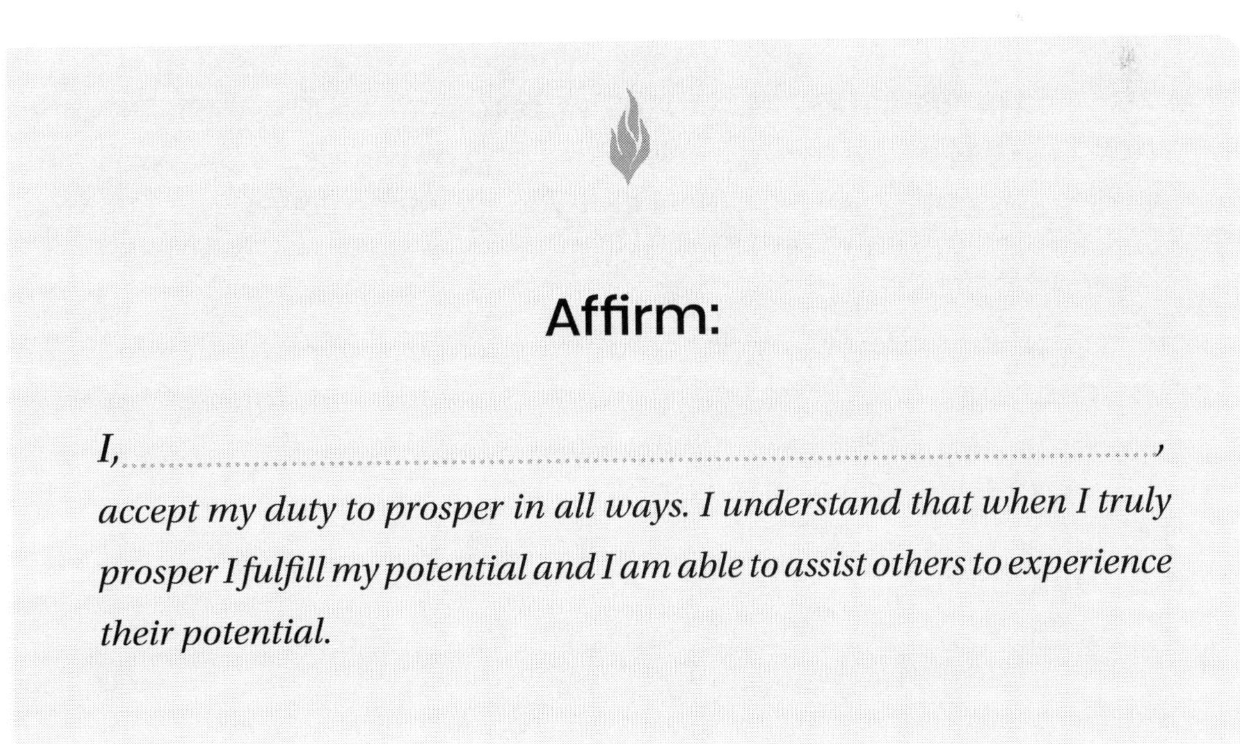

## Affirm:

*I, ..........................................................................................,*

*accept my duty to prosper in all ways. I understand that when I truly prosper I fulfill my potential and I am able to assist others to experience their potential.*

# ACTUALIZATION GUIDELINES

Expect unplanned good fortune to appear in your life sometime in the next seven days, and see what happens. When it happens, write a description of it here:

As soon as you can, remove from your life and environment everything that is not in line with your idea of living a truly prosperous life. List these things here and check them off as you eliminate them:

Don't wait to tithe and to invest a portion of your financial resources. Begin now and maintain a regular schedule of giving and investing.

## Write how you will do this:

***Think prosperous; feel prosperous; act prosperous!***

After meditation, and during the day when the thought comes to mind, identify with the inexhaustible ocean of fine energy which surrounds you and makes up the world in which you live. Remind yourself that this energy takes form and meets you at your level of need and acceptance. Know that life will never let you down.

If you are afraid of handling money because of the false idea that money is not good, or because you are afraid of the personal responsibility, learn to enjoy receiving and paying out money in a wise and prudent manner. After all, you are but handling a flow of energy, and to wisely handle energy flows is to live freely in this and all worlds. Be open to income and pay your just bills with gratitude. Be thankful that you are in the flow and that other people appreciate your services to them and that they trust you when giving you credit.

Always remember: things are not evidence of prosperity. Real prosperity is a matter of consciousness, and things are but an outer reflection of your own states of consciousness. True and lasting prosperity is your experience when you are in your right place in the cosmic scheme and when you are in an open flow of life.

## What Would You Do If...?

Yes, what would you do if you had all of the money, all of the resources, all of the talent and ability, right now, to engage in any useful project? Make a list. Then, on this and extra paper if needed, clearly write a comprehensive action-plan which could make possible the realization of your vision. As an aid to possibility-thinking, write your plans as if you were able to move ahead right now. Be sure to write down any useful ideas which come to mind as you list your plans and projects.

# GOAL ACHIEVEMENT PLAN

**Goal or Final Purpose:**

**Date For Completion/Achievement:**

I complete the purpose or achieve my goal by ______________________.

**Plans For Completion and/or Achievement:**

**Obstacles Or Restrictions, If Any:**

# SOLUTIONS AND PLANS OF ACTION:

*I use these plans and experience solutions.*

**Expected Benefits as a Result of Actualizing Plans**

## PURPOSES COMPLETED AND GOALS ACHIEVED:

**Completed/Achieved:**

Date:

**Completed/Achieved:**

Date:

**Completed/Achieved:**

Date:

*Record short-term gains and achievements as well as long-range ones.*

## GOAL OR FINAL PURPOSE

Use this page for personal notes, ideas, plans of action, or other useful purpose to enable yourself to be consciously involved with your program. You may wish to insert pictures or photos, clippings from published sources, or anything else that would assist your creative process.

## REVIEW

### True And Lasting Prosperity

*Clearly answer the following questions:*

**What does it mean to prosper?**

**Can any rational person learn to be prosperous?**

**What must be done before we can prosper?**

**Does fulfillment extend fully to this earth plane?**

- Why?

**Fear of success is one restriction common to many people.**

- List some more.

**Why do some people fear success?**

**What is the great essential in the cultivation of a prosperity consciousness?**

**What are a few things we can do to actualize the laws of success?**

**How can one find his area of real service?**

**Timeless thoughts to nourish the mind and refresh the soul ...**

# SECTION

## 7.[b]

## The Realization of Spiritual Perfection

# Definitions

**liberation of consciousness**: full enlightenment; elimination of any obstacles to complete knowledge-realization of God and of universal processes.

**Truth:** that which is so.

# THE REALIZATION OF SPIRITUAL PERFECTION

The realization of spiritual perfection is easy and natural. Easy, because we have only to turn our attention away from untruth and flow it to truth. Natural, because at the very center of our being we are already enlightened.

It is easy for a person who is willing to awaken to the realization of the true Self to do so because the soul is naturally inclined in the direction of awakening. It is the conditioned mind which causes one to feel dull and to yearn for involvement in confusing relationships and situations. All illumined teachers have emphasized the importance of turning attention to the source of life in order to consciously become aware of it. If one wants to know the truth about life and is willing to become attuned to the awakening process, the realization of spiritual perfection is possible in this current incarnation. When we meditate, we should inwardly know, *Pure consciousness is what I am.* This will result in correct Self-identification. If we think of ourselves as restricted, we are restricted; if we know ourselves to be unrestricted, we are free. We can take on faith what the illumined teachers tell us, and then make it our own through direct realization.

Never do we think in terms of improving upon our essential nature. Never do we think in terms of building a spiritual state of consciousness. That is because the soul is already complete, pure, and immortal, and this can be realized. Spiritual disciplines, of whatever tradition or form, are for the purpose of clearing the mental field, refining the nervous system, and rendering the physical body pure and responsive to the soul's needs. At times a person may ask *Why am I involved in spiritual practices if I am already a free being*? Spiritual practices cleanse the coverings of the soul (mental field and physical body) of impressions and restricting tendencies so that the soul can express freely as it was destined to express.

Truth is that which is so about life. It is not what one thinks is so, nor what one concludes to be so, but that which is so.

When we are functioning through a conditioned mental field, we are inclined to see only a partial view of our world, and we are inclined to miss the point even when we examine life carefully. Truth, Reality, is all about us and has only to be clearly perceived and acknowledged. Only when we have *ears to hear* and *eyes to see* can we know truth. When our awareness is restricted, when our faculties of discernment are clouded, we cannot know truth. Unbounded awareness and unveiled intelligence enable us to see what before eluded us. The truth about life can be known because, at the soul level, we already possess total understanding.

Knowing the truth frees the mind from bondage and from dependencies upon externals. Knowing the truth results in liberation of consciousness.

When we awaken to understanding, the concepts which formerly restricted us can be released. To be liberated is to be free, and to be free is to no longer be limited by concepts, attitudes, feelings or urges which are incompatible with the actualization of innate potential. A fully liberated person can function easily in any sphere and any environment in which he has a purpose for being. A liberated person is able to see opportunity all about him, and is able to make intelligent use of available resources in order to achieve his goals and fulfill his purposes. Neither age, general circumstances, or popular opinion can in any way restrict the soul which is open to the flow of life's goodness.

The realm of fulfillment exists now, and all can have access to it. We can live in the material world and still be aware of heaven. Heaven extends to all aspects and all levels of material manifestation.

Why is it that some people experience poverty and illness while others experience prosperity and health? Why is it that some people continue to remain in restricting circumstances even when the laws of mind and consciousness are widely known? A prosperous and healthy life is available to everyone. To blame past conditions or present circumstances is the way of weakness. One can begin where he is, and by applying the laws of mind and consciousness, open himself to see new reality worlds and experience them. The entire universe is made up of material substance. The fine energy of consciousness becomes subtle and then gross, but all expressions are from the source. This is why we affirm-There is one power, one presence and one substance in, through, and as the universe. We cannot blame karma for our circumstances as long as we know the way to freedom. The past cannot be changed, but our present patterns can be changed. Our present attitude can be adjusted. Our way of looking at life can be altered. We can invite new and desirable circumstances into our lives if we are open to the possibility, and if we are willing to make inner changes to allow it to happen. Every person who learns to live in harmony with the laws of nature experiences fulfillment in every area of his life experience. It is a matter of personal responsibility and willingness to do what needs to be done to allow transformation and change.

There is a pure realm, a non-dual realm, which remains ever the same. This pure realm is the cause and support of all outer manifestation. Extending itself as the cosmic soul, life appears as a self-involved electrical field with full awareness. The cosmic soul is innately possessed of eternal being, total intelligent consciousness, and endless power.

Life is forever, it is eternal. Life has no beginning and it has no end. Influences which result in outer conditions begin and end, but the dance of life is forever and ever. We are forever and ever because we are units of the cosmic soul. The intelligent power pervading the universe is referred to as the *lord of the universe*. Really, the cosmic soul is our larger true Self, as the ocean is the larger true reality of the wave. We can experience our larger true Self during occasions of transcendence and during deep meditation when the mental waves are stilled. We can, while inwardly clear, contemplate the nature of the cosmic soul and comprehend the reality of it and how the world process takes place. Everything can be known to one who learns to contemplate correctly.

The tendencies toward brightness, activity, and gravity exist in the cosmic soul and make possible the manifestations of the universes, the movements leading to evolutionary change, and final world redemption.

The tendencies toward brightness, activity and gravity exist within each person, also. When we surrender to the inclination in the direction of brightness, we tread the spiritual path and we are open to the possibility of full enlightenment. When we harness the tendency in the direction of activity, we are able to set and achieve goals easily and to satisfy our just desires. When we are compelled by the tendency in the direction of activity, without reason, we are restless and in motion without purpose. When we are dominated by the tendency in the direction of gravity, we become overcome with heaviness, inertia, and dullness. We can easily do what is useful to our enlightenment purpose by becoming aware of our thoughts, feelings, attitudes, relationships and actions. Whatever results in brightness and greater awareness is useful; whatever results in confusion and unconsciousness is not useful. We do not have to struggle with thoughts of rightness and wrongness relative to our thoughts, feelings, relationships, and actions. Whatever leads us in the direction of cosmic consciousness and contributes to a healthier world condition is useful. By adopting useful thoughts, feelings, attitudes, relationships, and actions, we soon find that we are in harmony with the energies of the universe, and prosperity and fulfillment are easily experienced. To prosper is to thrive, to flourish, to be successful. Life thrives, life flourishes, life is successful. We should be like this. We can be like this when we are open to life's natural inclination in the direction of fulfillment. World consciousness is being purified, and we can contribute to this cleansing by seeing to our own enlightenment and liberation.

The holy spirit, the directing force of the cosmic soul, shines on the moving creative energy extending from the cosmic soul, and the Word is made manifest. The Word emerges from the cosmic soul and extends into and as the universal process.

The intelligence of the cosmic soul influences the energy flowing from the cosmic soul, and thus matter is directed and enlivened. This is why we affirm that one thing appears as all things. We are ever relating to the one essence which is appearing as all forms about us. Because the universal process is intelligently directed, there is a plan and a purpose to the process. When we are attuned to this grand purpose we experience effortless awakening and fulfillment. When we attempt to work against this process we experience pain. It may not seem just that people who lack knowledge of the process experience pain, but these people can be taught the way to awakening and they, too, can know the truth about life. All souls, sooner or later, will awaken and know the truth. There is a supportive influence built into the universal process. This is why it cannot do anything but continue along a predestined pattern. The planet will not be destroyed by any of man's whims or because of his lack of understanding. We are experiencing a planetary emergence of superconscious influence which is causing people to awaken and to become more attentive to the needs of each other and to the needs of the planet. Crisis and conflict result in confrontation and change. This is an effect of evolutionary motion, which is certain to result in harmony and balance for nature and for all people.

The substance of the manifest worlds is made up of creative energy, light particles, space and time. God, as the primal fabric, extends as the worlds. Behind this substance of which forms are made is the realm of the gods, the shining (illumined) beings. Corning through this primal substance the gods are known as man. Awakening from material identification, man knows once again his pure nature, and experiences the realization of spiritual perfection.

Creative energy, light particles, space and time represent the field which makes all manifestation possible. All things emerge from this field and all things flow back into it. It is inexhaustible; therefore, thinking in terms of limitation is folly. All that one needs for fulfilled living is already provided, once it can be seen and utilized. We have but to open our eyes to available good, and to renounce all attitudes and concepts of the mind which prevent clear perception. Spiritual education is required of all people who do not understand these principles. Spiritual education should begin at an early age before concepts are firmly set in the field of the mind. But it is never too late. No matter how long one has retained false concepts, these can be released in a moment once clear insight has been experienced. The mental darkness of thousands of years can be banished when the light of the soul invades the mind. Our true home is inner space. We have come from inner space and we shall return to inner space when our sojourn on planet Earth is over. We can retire to this inner space any time during meditation and prayerful contemplation. By so doing, we can be refreshed, and then return to the sphere of relative duties and perform with greater effectiveness and superconscious influence. The world in which we live is the testing ground where we try ourselves and learn to use the laws of mind and consciousness. In this way we experience the actualization of soul potential. Life works through us to assist in the evolutionary process and to bring about needed change. When understood, the universal process is entirely benevolent.

There is no independent universe, and there is no individual person. The universe is an extension of primal being, the result of outflowing force acted upon by innate intelligence. The seeming individual person is but a viewpoint of the cosmic soul. These viewpoints appear on the surface of manifest nature as waves appear on the surface of water. The cosmic soul is both the wave and the ocean.

When we think of the universe as a creation *out of nothing* we are in error. The universe was formed out of *something* which seems to be without characteristics. The absolute, the *void*, is really pure consciousness which contains, in dormant condition, all of the potential expressed outwardly in nature. Sound has an origin. Anything that is, has an origin and is not separate from the origin. The universe is, then, the body of the cosmic soul. Since we are specialized viewpoints of the cosmic soul, we are not, and have never been, separate from the source. The sense of being separate, the ego sense, is the cause of unknowing. When true knowing is experienced, we see the truth that the cosmic soul is our larger true Self and that we have always been bright and free at the soul level.

Mind pervades the material universe. There is but one mind; that which appears as individualized mind is but a fragment of the one mind. Through this particularization of mind, used by the soul, full conscious cooperation between man and God is possible. That is, we can learn to work in harmony with the evolutionary process when we are open to the possibility.

To work with the evolutionary process is what is meant as doing God's will. How do we find God's will for ourselves? Through prayer, meditation, and purification, and by being open to guidance. Even when we do not know how to act or what to do, we can prepare ourselves by doing whatever is at hand with full attention and with the best use of our abilities. In this way we become proficient, and we are able to meet opportunity when it surfaces, and be fully responsible. If we are not prepared when opportunity is presented, we will not be able to fully perform our duties. The pattern, then, is to plan for higher duties and to wait for opportunity. Enlightenment teachers assert that the universe floats in the mind of the cosmic soul. Therefore, they say that the world process is God's dream. It is subject to change and transformation, but the original cause was the urge of the cosmic soul to express.

Subtle aura-electricities are the causes of material appearances. Interacting, they manifest as the electric realm or astral realm. More fully extending, they appear as the physical universe. The universe, on all levels, from subtle to gross, is really a play of lights and shadows, a forever-occurring unfoldment against the screen of time and space.

The gross physical worlds are not firm and unyielding. They are forever changing. No thing is the same from instant to instant. Outer change may not be discernible, but inner change is always taking place. Heaven and earth will pass away, only to be sent forth again, because this is how it is with the life process. Enlightened man can call forth from the sea of fine energy any form he can envision. By this process, he can adjust his personal world and assist others to live more easily, and more in harmony with their destined ends. Working with fine forces is not so much a matter of will, as it is the ability to see and accept. In other words, a person of pure faith can produce seeming miracles by understanding the true nature of the world in which he lives.

As the cosmic soul is superior to the one mind and, through the one mind, superior to universal manifestation, so the soul is superior to particularized mind and to personal environment. The universe is a reflection of inner causes, and material bodies are reflections of inner causes and states. Mental influence extends into material forms or bodies.

Outer forms are modified by changes at subtle levels. The physical body of man is rendered healthy or diseased by mental and emotional states and conditions. A well-ordered mind and a harmonious emotional life reflect as health of body. Confusion at mental and emotional levels can reflect as disease of the body.

By altering states of consciousness and mental attitudes, man can live creatively and freely in the world. By awakening from the dream of mortality, the soul consciously experiences its real nature. This is enlightenment. With the enlightenment experience, the light of the soul floods mind and body with cleansing influence. The experience of fulfillment on earth is then natural and effortless.

We have the freedom of choice relative to the mental attitude we entertain. We can decide to be happy or we can decide to be sad. We can decide to look at the world with optimism or we can choose to see only difficulty and trouble. Through practice, we can learn to remain conscious, always. We can learn to sleep at will, awaken at will, and enter into the meditative experience at will. We can even learn to dream consciously, and to use superior powers of creative visualization for intended purposes. The dream of mortality is the illusion that we are mortal, material, and destined to end at death of the body. When we experience illumination, the mind is filled with light and is cleansed of all destructive patterns, tendencies, and habits. This light of the superconscious flows through the nervous system and refines it. It flows into the body and stops the process of decay. In time, an enlightened person functions through a purified and glorified body for the duration of his life on earth. When destiny has been fulfilled, a conscious being departs the body easily. This, too, is a natural process when the occasion is appropriate.

By clearly understanding that only one life exists, we can flow with the natural trends and live by grace. By such understanding and by such experience, we are in harmony with a supportive universe, every person we meet becomes our friend, and the forces of nature attend to our needs.

Grace is *the activity of the holy spirit moving and expressing through us to transform and regenerate*. When we live without fear and without any feeling of distrust, the universe proves to be supportive of all our useful intentions. It is as though the power of the cosmic ocean were behind us, and we know the power is not original with the ego-sense but is the power of the larger true Self. Experiencing total freedom in this world, we then know that total freedom will be ours in all worlds.

The soul is already healthy and prosperous. It is the nature of the soul to thrive, to flourish and to be successful, just as it is the nature of the cosmic soul to thrive, to flourish, and to fulfill intended purposes. A conscious being does not need to try to be happy, healthy, and prosperous because happiness, health, and prosperity are completely natural. Unhappiness, sickness and limitation are evidence of lack of total soul-awareness.

Wherever there is limitation in our lives, there we will find need for examination and cleansing. We should experience health in all areas of our lives: spiritual, mental, emotional, and physical, and in relationships. We should experience freedom to move through the material worlds without restrictions. Any limitation is evidence of need for awakening and for actualizing soul-qualities in harmony with a larger design.

The fulfillment of soul-destiny is assured, just as the fulfillment of God's plan for the transformation of the universe is assured. There is nothing to fear; all things work together for ultimate good and this is clearly seen when the inner eye is opened.

The inner eye is the faculty of intuitive perception. When the intuitive ability is unveiled, we see life for what it is, and there are no longer any unanswered questions. Whenever fearful, be reminded: *Let not your heart be troubled, neither let it be afraid*. Be at peace because there is a master plan even now unfolding which will assure ultimate good for all beings.

The seeming stages of soul unfoldment are but degrees of natural awakening. One does not develop or build a spiritual consciousness; one awakens to the realization of spiritual perfection.

As the organs of perception are unveiled, one by one, we appear to ascend the ladder to final knowledge. We awaken to the next level as we learn our lessons at the present level, and as a result of yearning to know the truth. To live a simple life, a life in harmony with natural laws, and to yearn for soul-realization all of the time is the way to accelerated awakening and enlightenment. When we are surrendered to the evolutionary inclination of life (the will of God) we find that our progress is more rapid. We are then carried along by a dynamic flow, and this is referred to as being caught up in the love of God. The more we surrender ego-sense in favor of becoming aware of our higher true Self, the more quickly we awaken and come into our true place in the divine order.

The force that consciously powers the universe can be known and experienced as a benevolent, supportive urge in the direction of completion. This is the assurance of fulfillment in all spheres, planes, and dimensions.

We emphasize the possibility of fulfillment in this present incarnation, in this present world, because there is no value in waiting until some future time or space condition before we become fully conscious. The more conscious we are, right where we are, the more free we are and the more value we have to the ongoing evolutionary process. Service to others and our world is vital to our awakening because, without service, there is the tendency for one to be selfish and self-centered. The ideal is to be expansive and to become cosmic conscious. Other planes, dimensions, and spheres are also inhabited by souls who are conscious, confused, and unconscious, just as we find them here in our present world. There will never be a more opportune time than the moment to decide to awaken and to be free.

“ ”

***Firm in the realization of spiritual perfection, one is forever serene and fulfilled.***

Behind the manifest realm is that pure essence which remains ever the same. Behind man's feeling nature and behind the processes of thought, is that pure essence which remains ever the same. This pure essence is known during occasions of settled meditation and during occasions of clear Self-awareness. Established in this awareness one knows, *I am conscious, I am immortal, I am the discerning witness to all that transpires about me.*

An enlightened person is not vague, strange, or out of contact with the realm in which his destiny calls him to function. An enlightened person functions clearly in the present moment while being inwardly settled in perfect understanding. An enlightened person is healthy, sane, and fully functional. An enlightened person performs all duties with patient understanding, and his presence in the world is the occasion for a stream of blessing to flow into it.

All that man seeks in his various endeavors is experienced in pure form when enlightenment is experienced. Even when enlightened, one may attend to duties because of motiveless necessity. That is, one does what must be done, but there is no personal motive for such action or involvement. The conscious being works as the cosmic soul works, because it is the nature of life to express as long as expression is the inclination. When the inclination is no longer present, there is rest. A conscious being does not try to figure this out; such a one merely does what must be done with perfect grace and appropriate usefulness.

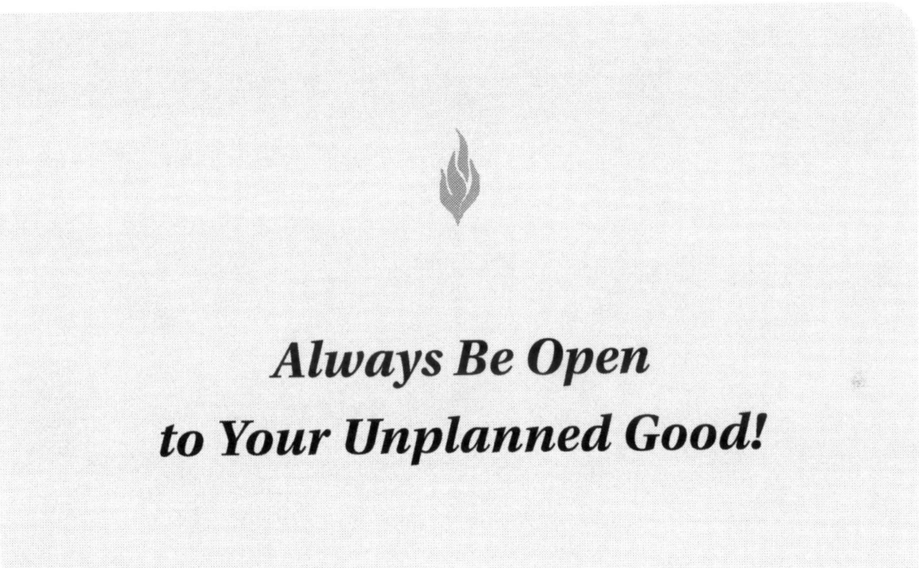

Made in the USA
Columbia, SC
14 March 2024

33021424R00248